PASSPORT TO A
MILLION DOLLARS

How to Book Your Ticket to Wealth

By Adam N. Herod, M.Ed.

ADAM N. HEROD, M.ED.

Dedication

This book is dedicated to my colleagues, the 75% of America working to have investable assets to grow wealth. You are the backbone of America, and you deserve all the best in your working and retirement years. If this book even reaches half of you, we will be heading in the right direction.

And to my wife, who is the epitome of everything we should be in order to succeed and prosper in life.

ADAM N. HEROD, M.ED.

Preface

The intention of this book – besides aiming to benefit your overall financial outlook and, in turn, your life – is to get its readers to build a community and start a conversation.

First, with yourself: "Have I been doing it right when it comes to earning, saving and investing?" And second, with your financial institution and the advisor that represents it.

"Do they have my best interests in mind? If they do not then who would?"

There are few greater callings in life than to raise the consciousness of others. This book aims to do just that.

As an educator, I will circle back upon ideas in order to gain mastery over our subject matter of personal finance and wealth. But I will keep it concise enough to not drawl on and lose your interest.

In raising your consciousness regarding your personal wealth attainment, it will hopefully benefit you in ways you did not expect.

At the time of publication, I am on the very path you are – becoming a millionaire. This is very different from the authors who have already made it and are reaching down to pull others up.

We are on this mountain together - side-by-side - making tangible steps in the right direction.

Everything in this book comes from others who are wealthy. It is a conglomerate of sorts, tapping into some of the best moves required to make it up that million-dollar mountain – or beyond!

Although it is angled toward the middle class and uses a number of examples from the field of education, there are a lot of people working in America that could benefit from the principles in this book.

It is from the learned and accomplished in finance that we will learn to climb for ourselves, regardless of profession.

Using their collective knowledge and the wayfinding of experts, we will look to accomplish this very meaningful challenge for ourselves and our families.

We will share as a community and grow together **@themilliondollareducator**.

And one day, when we stand at the top of the mountain and feel the sunshine, we can work to be a beacon for others.

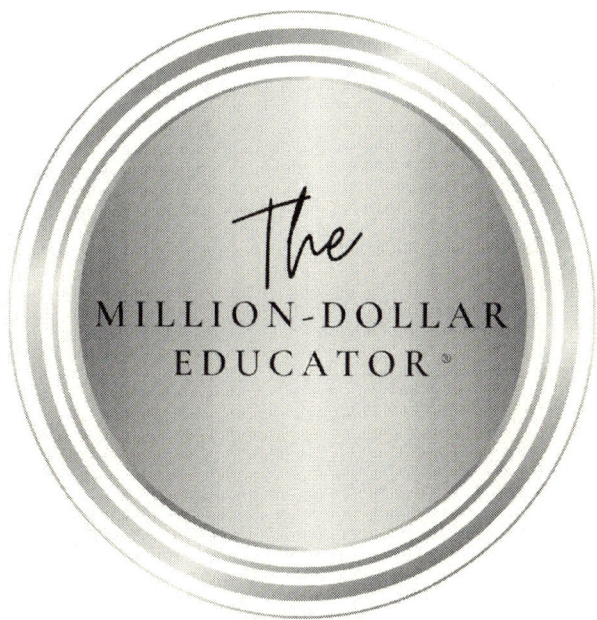

CONTENTS

ADAM N. HEROD, M.ED.

UNIT 1
INTRODUCTION

Case Study: Teacher Retirement in America

The financial wellbeing of teachers – and, frankly, all who invest for retirement - is a national concern.

Specifically, the system that comprises the sale of retirement plans and the investments provided to Main Street America, is one that acts to sap the wealth attainment potential of our nation's hardest working employees.

Worse yet, nobody - especially your financial advisor - wants you to know.

For example, every year nearly 3.8 million teachers across the country face an uphill battle regarding their personal finances, especially in retirement.

Set aside the argument on teacher salaries and total compensation to home in on the retirement planning provided for teachers, and, unfortunately, you will find a myriad of issues.

Let's start with the fact that the general population of America is woefully prepared for retirement.

Not just teachers, everyone.

You did not come here for dismal statistics, so I will not hit you with them all the time; however, it serves the point that most of us - about 75% - lack investable assets for stock market plays, including mutual funds, ETFs, individual stocks and, if you dare, cryptocurrencies.

The shutdown for COVID-19 and its variants brought a number of new, short-term, HODL (Hold on for Dear Life) investors into play.

But for the purposes of this book, we will investigate the long-term, strategic retirement planning we have control over: the 401(k), 403(b) or 457(b) and traditional or Roth IRAs.

One of the factors educators must consider – and inevitably you if you're a corporate employee - is the choice you have in retirement plans outside of your core account.

Teachers start with a pension, but where do they go after that?

You might have a 401(k), but where do you go?

Although 90% of public-school educators are enrolled in a pension, TeacherPensions.org reported that over half of teachers leave the career without a pension, and those that do only earn in the range of $20,000 to $40,000 per year.

Only one jurisdiction cleared $50,000 overall, Washington D.C.

For most, a pension will simply not cover their needs.

How about those with a workplace 401(k) plan?

Do they fare any better?

Sadly, most do not.

And most were automatically enrolled and do not know their full contribution amount.

So where does one turn?

Ideally, your district or company will offer a few options for supplemental retirement savings, which can include Roth 401(k)s for corporate folks, and 403(b)s and 457(b)s for educators and state employees.

We can also look outside of our employers for after-tax investments, including IRAs and Roth IRAs.

But your employer is tasked with choosing plans and annuities that are most beneficial to you; however, we often find that many of these plans have standards in place to make the financial institution and its advisors more money - often at the expense of the employee.

The book titled, *Where Are All the Customers' Yachts? Or a Good Hard Look at Wall Street* explains it all.

Quite literally, an industry was designed to allow advisors - reference "salespersons" - to earn income from your elected investments, all while they sit behind computers and conduct check-ins with 20-hour work weeks.

Before I dig in too much on advisors, know that there are truly great people out there helping others; however, it is the industry and the laws that allow for decisions benefiting the salespeople and their institutions that must be unveiled.

You see, the advisors handing out donuts and coffee in your staff lounge earn money from an Assets Under Management (AUM) system, on top of bonuses and commissions from the sale of financial products.

Let's say you bring a new advisor a $500,000 account that you've been working on for over 25 years - tirelessly saving as much as possible month after month after month.

After you sign on the dotted line, your advisor will make a commission that will trigger as soon as you sign.

That's one form of compensation.

Then, while he or she watches over your account the advisor could earn up to 1% on the principal amount in your account.

1% of $500,000 is $5,000.

He or she will earn that every year, and even more if your account grows.

If an advisor manages 100 such accounts, he or she would be earning $500,000 per year.

Not too bad.

But have you seen any one of your peers earning half a million per year?

I didn't think so.

What's a 403(b) or 401(k)?

It's likely the plans being sold to you and your peers fall under the category of a 403(b) or 403(b) annuity.

Those employed in the corporate world are often automatically enrolled in their employer's 401(k) program, with a minimum of 3% contributing each month into a standard target-date-fund.

But those in education must seek out further investment opportunities, especially if they desire more money in retirement than the pension.

In comes the 403(b).

If you haven't caught up to inform yourself on the 403(b) yet, here is a quick explanation from Investopedia.com.

A 403(b) plan is a retirement plan for specific employees of public schools, tax-exempt organizations and certain ministries. These plans can invest in either annuities or mutual funds.

A 403(b) plan is also another name for a tax-sheltered annuity plan, and the features of a 403(b) plan are comparable to those found in a 401(k) plan.

A 403(b) plan allows you to place money into a 401(k)-like account prior to taxes being assessed.

This is known as a pre-tax or tax-advantaged account.

These plans are great for those that would more likely spend any extra income leftover from their paychecks.

Contributing to a 403(b) or 401(k) also decreases the taxable portion of the income you will have at the end of the year, so you'll owe less in overall taxes that year.

Money set aside for a 403(b) can grow and act as part of a balanced retirement plan at the end of your career, when it will finally be taxed upon retirement.

Not Without Its Problems | The Fee Nightmare

In an article titled, *"Think your retirement plan is bad? Talk to a teacher,"* Tara Siegel Barnard of the New York Times investigated a very specific issue regarding these plans - fees.

She found out that anyone not able to invest in a 401(k) plan, including: teachers, clergy members, members of religious institutions, nonprofits and charities is invested in a 403(b) plan that was costing the entire U.S. investor base over $10 billion a year in unnecessary management fees.

10 billion dollars on the backs of our nation's educators for fees that benefit the financial institutions and their salespeople.

And are 401(k) investors completely shielded?

Not entirely.

Think of how many hours a week you put into your work.

Why should a single penny of your hard-earned money, that you set aside for a financially secure future, be taken away by the very financial institution you decided to trust - just so they can pay commissions and bonuses to their advisors and line their own pockets?

The reason rests in loose regulations governing 403(b) programs, within which we *should* invest but be more careful with whom we trust to oversee the accounts.

… more on trustworthy firms later.

How is this scenario allowed?

Whereas 401(k) investment programs are governed under the Employee Retirement Income Security Act of 1974, 403(b) funds for educators and others do not fall under these protections.

The act was originally set in place to protect American employees of corporations, but those that work in the public sector are left unprotected.

How does this manifest to damage your wealth attainment?

Plainly put, advisors are not required to act in your best interests.

But even though they should act in your best interests, imagine defining "best interests."

There's a lot of gray.

So in the case of educators, institutions that provide 403(b) annuities to teachers - often denoted by fancy looking acronyms and represented by highly commissioned "advisors" - are actually insurance companies with salespeople offering high-cost alternatives and promises of returns that often underperform customer-centric institutions such as Fidelity, Vanguard and Schwab.

The latter group of institutions specializes in low-cost retirement funds and does not employ salespeople, so hardworking people like you and me can realize our retirement goals without funding someone else's yacht.

Best Customer-Oriented Investment Firms

Best for Personal Finance: Vanguard
Best for ETFs: Charles Schwab
Best for IRAs: Fidelity

Benzinga.com

What's the Problem with Fees?

The issues we face are multifaceted and highly clandestine on the part of the insurance and annuity providers.

This isn't to say that all funds within customer-centric institutions are without some tradeoffs either, but there can be opportunities to cut fees without sacrificing performance – of which we should truly consider when trying to reach our retirement goals.

We must become informed investors, and you are already on your way.

You see, insurance companies that provide workplace retirement plans for teachers have developed 403(b) products that skew the benefits toward them, not necessarily their clients.

These products make the providers millions in convoluted transaction costs, tax costs, redemption fees, management fees, exchange fees, purchase fees and more which they charge back to the client.

They can make transactions within funds without permission, and whether the fund increases or decreases in value you will foot the bill.

These actions pull money out of your account little by little over time, sucking the air out of what should be your ever-expanding retirement balloon.

Why would they do that?

Well, get this!

Legally, they can advertise little to no overall fees but some have been found to charge $6,000 or more *per year* in overall costs to a client account.

In fees alone, $6,000 may be more than many of us can put in our accounts in a given year.

Think the problem isn't widespread?

Check out the small list of news headlines below, all regarding teacher retirement in the form of high cost 403(b)s.

"Are You Getting Ripped Off With Your 403(b) Retirement Plan?" – Investor Junkie, 2019

"Why These Teacher Retirement Plans Aren't Making the Grade." – CNBC, 2018

"How Not to Save for Retirement If You Are a Teacher." TeachforAmerica.org, 2018

"Some 403(b) Plan Advice for Teachers" – ABC News, 2011

Some investors discover their mistakes early and make changes as they gain more knowledge of the industry.

In one case, a teacher had signed up for a 403(b) plan that promised a 2% return.

We all know what to do when we hear promises, right?

He, likely, enjoyed the idea of a guarantee, but quickly realized he had missed out when the market had returned 12% over the five-year period he had been investing.

The cost of the "guarantee" robbed him of $8,000 in growth in that short amount of time.

Guess who got to keep the other returns?

You guessed it – the financial institution.

The couple that had been charged $6,000 in investment fees had $250,000 in their 403(b) account.

Mathematically, this charge represents 2.4% of their overall account value.

This is an erosion of wealth that is simply unacceptable, because we have better options.

Options with much lower overall fees, and - oftentimes - similar fund makeup.

What Can We Do?

Everything you are reading is real and legal under our current system.

So what do we do?

A young Elon Musk once said, "Really, the only thing that makes sense is to strive for great collective enlightenment."

Your advisor will be prepared to combat the awareness you will gain.

They are ready to say canned responses such as, "Well, our returns will be better than if you managed the account on your own."

And, "We have some of the highest returns in the industry."

For those of you who have a long relationship with a financial advisor, have they ever ventured to ask if you are ready to increase your contributions?

Of course, they have!

That's because they stand to make more money in fees as your total account value grows.

We *should* increase our contributions each year to beat inflation, but shouldn't *you* be making more money as your account grows?

Now, if you are ready to pull all your investments and throw them into a savings account - or worse, yet, put it all under your mattress - you have the wrong idea.

It is not likely that anyone would suggest keeping your money out of the market.

You just have to find the options that work best for you, overall.

Just like stocks, there are good companies and bad companies.

In retirement investments such as 403(b)s and 401(k)s, there are good providers and bad providers, as well as good funds and bad funds.

At the end of the day, we know that investing for retirement is not terribly complicated; however, insurance providers offering 403(b) investment products to teachers have made their offerings terribly convoluted, so we feel like unwitting peasants in their lofty cash kingdom.

What's to say about your 401(k)?

There are ways around this, and the good news is that by the end of this book you will more likely be able to choose an advisor and better vet them or take the reins yourself - should you choose to do so.

Not only will we analyze what is going on in the retirement industry, especially as it relates to teachers, but we will examine ways to take back your financial future.

Remember, replace 403(b) with 401(k) in this book and a lot of the same principles and concerns will apply.

Whether you are a new teacher or working for a Fortune 500, the goal is to enlighten and empower you to ask the right questions and make a change to improve your overall retirement outlook, without making others rich in the process.

A small book purchase might end up saving you tens of thousands in fees, while teaming you up with more customer-friendly institutions.

Imagine the outcomes.

Going Deeper | A System-Wide Issue

Let's continue our case study by analyzing teacher pay and compensation.

Benefits overall can make teaching a desirable career in many states and counties; however, the wealth potential and the security that might normally come with a defined benefit plan, like a pension, are not equitable across the country.

According to the Economic Policy Institute, teachers are paid less than other career employees with similar education levels and skills, even when factoring in benefits such as a pension and healthcare.

For teachers, total compensation was 11% less than other comparable workers, and it was determined teacher pay was 17% less overall when salary was singled out.

We know teacher pay is lower than comparable peers, so why rehash this notion in a book about personal finance and teacher retirement planning?

We must establish that every dollar counts.

If it is ours and we are choosing to invest in our futures, why should we allow trained salespeople acting as financial advisors to fund their lifestyles while we put our noses to the grindstone?

Further, 40% of public-school teachers are not covered by social security benefits.

Many states opted out of social security for its public workers, hoping to emphasize saving into a state benefit plan they'd develop and manage on their own. If you live in one of the following states and you are a teacher, you may not qualify for social security: Alaska, California, Connecticut, Georgia (some areas), Illinois, Kentucky (some areas), Louisiana, Maine, Massachusetts, Missouri, Nevada, Ohio, Rhode Island, and Texas.

Regardless of whether you fit our case study or you're in a corporation with a 401(k), upon analyzing **The Ultimate Plan** you will have a better idea of how to specifically meet your goals.

But promise you won't skip ahead, as there's so much value in the coming pages.

Consulting with a certified, fee-only advisor is always recommended, as no one can lay claim to a one-size-fits all plan.

All variables for retirement must be considered, and no two households are alike.

Beyond social security benefits, public school teachers are often lauded for having access to a defined benefit plan like the pension.

Especially, when workers in many other industries watched their pension plans go extinct, putting a greater responsibility on their shoulders to contribute to their 401(k).

When people mention a pension, they might think of income for life.

For many early teachers, that was likely the case as their tiers and bargaining units developed benefits that experienced outstanding market conditions.

But since the crash of 2008, pension systems have become strained.

Employees are living longer and the projections the states used did not factor in for realistic market returns.

Basically, they calculated blissful outcomes with only ideal market conditions.

Over time, pension systems asked more from their working employees to make up for their miscalculations, requiring more to come out of their paychecks, while providing less in overall income for those already in retirement.

Since 90% of teachers are enrolled in pension plans, it is once again important to highlight the reality that many pension plans did not provide more than $50,000 in overall income per year.

A Brookings.edu study scaled out even further and noted that across the country $500 billion worth of defined benefit plans were represented by unfunded liabilities.

Plainly speaking, the plans will not be able to afford $500 billion in what they promised their employees.

That's a major shortfall.

But, again, we are working on understanding the concerns surrounding the systems that have been put in place and marketed to us.

That way we can better understand how to better our own financial futures.

We Are Partially to Blame

Generally, when it comes to personal finances and retirement planning, we wait too long to act.

Either:

> (a) we bury our heads in the sand and ignore everything we need to discuss - known as **The Ostrich Effect.**

> (b) we do not have time to handle these topics

> OR

> (c) we simply do not care to learn because it is too daunting or stressful

Then, some make the mistake of talking to a retirement counselor or fee-based advisor only one year prior to retirement only to find out we could have set ourselves up better.

Ideally, conversations about how much to save and which plans to choose should happen in our twenties and thirties, while final check-ins with our retirement counselors should happen fifteen, ten and at the least five years prior to retiring.

Along the way, who is going to tell you your 401(k) or 403(b) has been off axis?

Who is going to dig deep into the intricacies of your account to see what can be improved?

So the system runs unchecked, except for a small number of folks willing to dig deeper and take care of themselves, and better yet speak up to inform others.

Our lack of financial education hampers us.

The wealthy invest and grow their money, while those of us in the middle class look to buy items that depreciate over time, such as cars and clothes.

Often, we have money left over to invest, but it is a matter of determining where in our budgets to cut back or where we can go to earn more to make our dreams a reality.

If you do not have a dream, you will soon enough.

The Gift Wrapping Isn't Free

The investment packages we are sold by advisors are a bundled offering of stocks and funds that are marketed as "managed" so that we feel taken care of.

"We manage it for you," they say.

"Phew, I can go back to doing what I do best and let you handle the big money stuff," we confide.

And there the advisor goes smiling all the way to the bank.

We must remember the offerings provided by some advisors can include annuity packages – especially those with 403(b)s. The annuity packages have the same general stock/equity recipe provided by mutual funds in customer-centric providers, except for one major detail.

The companies they represent package a group of funds together and place what's called a wrapper around them to charge more fees.

It's like buying pre-packaged oranges and paying an excessive price for the packaging, while the a-la-carte options are fresher, yet cheaper and don't skimp on quality.

We fall for this trick across the consumption and investment spectrum.

When we evaluate the two funds in this next example, we must first recognize the fees charged.

Vanguard, a customer-centric fund provider, offers a passive index fund that comprises the top 500 companies in the United States and charges 0.04%.

An investor contributing to a Vanguard S&P 500 fund would be able to tap into the power of U.S. growth and only have $40 charged for every $100,000 he or she invested in a given year.

This is about as low as fees will get, even though there are some zero fee funds.

It will help you to understand that an index fund, which tracks the S&P 500 for example, is self-cleansing, meaning that if a company cannot remain as one of the top 500 in the United States, the fund no longer recognizes it - relegating the fund out of its holdings.

Effectively, this allows an investor to very easily ensure they have access to the best companies in the United States in any given year.

Inevitably, the downfall of a company and a delisting from the S&P 500 will be buoyed by the fact that the majority are growing and benefiting both the index fund and your bottom line.

Top 10 Companies in VOYA's Corporate Leaders 100 Fund *As of Spring 2021 Expenses: Max of 5.75%	Top 10 Companies in Vanguard's S&P 500 Fund *As of Spring 2021 Expenses: 0.04%
Includes: Apple Inc., Microsoft Corp., Amazon.com Inc., Alphabet Inc., Facebook Inc., Berkshire Hathaway Inc., JPMorgan Chase & Co, Johnson & Johnson, Visa. Fund invests 1% in each of the 100 companies in the S&P 100 Index.	Includes: Apple Inc., Microsoft Corp., Amazon.com Inc., Alphabet Inc., Facebook Inc., Tesla Inc., Berkshire Hathaway Inc., JPMorgan Chase & Co., Johnson & Johnson, Visa Inc.

If the top 500 companies in the United States are too few and too regionalized for your taste, there are even total market funds that tap into the best companies across the planet.

This adds even more layers of protection against risk.

So not only are fees extremely low in an index fund, you also have access to a fluid, ever-adapting investment that includes the top companies over your investing lifetime.

On the other hand, as a comparison, the actively managed VOYA fund is one that specifically selects the top 100 companies in the S&P index; however, it charges a maximum of 5.75% in total fees.

When looking at the initial information on their website, VOYA publishes a 0.52% overall fee.

This looks to be quite low, but in the world of passive index investing this is actually much higher than what is usually offered.

VOYA's account is an example of an actively managed fund.

Look a little closer again and they publish the fund's returns over a given year.

For the Year-to-Date (YTD) return in 2021, the fund was up 13.94%, but after total fees you get a return of 7.37%.

If inflation averaged 2% for the year, then you only gained a 5% return on your investment.

Get ready, because a 5.75% total fee on $100,000 would cost you a total of $5,750.

You mean I have to pay more in fees for less than average performance?

More people are doing this than you realize, and in our case study of educators over two-thirds of America's teachers are enrolled in high-cost annuities.

While Digging Holes

When I was 18, I used my last summer at home to work as a landscaper for a large contractor in the Finger Lakes region of New York State.

My father had instilled in me the notion of beginning my earning years as soon as possible, so I could take advantage of the compounding growth my retirement investments would achieve over time.

But something in me said I needed to get my butt kicked for a summer before I went to college and eventually took a desk job.

There'd be no gap year to figure out what I wanted to do with my life, I'd prove to myself the value of my education and get to work right out of college with perspective and vigor.

My dad had just endured some rocky years working as a corporate accountant and had taken an early buyout package to disassociate himself from the tightening corporate culture.

From what I had witnessed, business was *not* the right environment for me.

So I signed up to work like a dog under the hot summer sun.

While some of my friends got to ride around on mowers every day, I was put on a planting crew.

I remember waking up at 5:30 AM every morning feeling like I'd only taken a 30-minute nap.

My body ached, my skin was burned, and I couldn't eat enough food or drink enough water.

When I worked alongside some of my new friends, who were from Mexico, Guatemala, and other South American countries, they would often ask what I planned to study in college.

I remember telling them I wanted to become a lawyer. Then they'd ask the obvious question - what the heck I was doing out on a landscaping crew.

In truth, there was something I needed to prove to myself.

I needed to prove that going to college was the right move.

Boy, I sure got all the proof I needed.

When I sat in my college classes, I often thought about that long, hard summer.

I didn't miss it much.

I wanted to distance myself as far from that life as possible.

My dad reminded me I'd have opportunities far beyond what an hourly wage could provide, including:

- a higher overall salary
- greater choices within my career
- retirement and health benefits
- and less strenuous work, overall

This perspective fueled me and still gives me an appreciation for my work with my students today.

The neatest thing that happened to me that summer was a statement I received summarizing all that I earned.

I was able to put up over $6,500 in hourly wages and overtime, and $1,500 in retirement.

Retirement?!

I was utterly confused at this figure.

So I asked, "Dad, why did they put money in for retirement? I was never going to retire from there!"

Having moved around the business world a few times and being self-taught in the basics of investing, my Dad knew enough about personal finance that he was able to avoid paying someone to manage his money.

Avoiding that 1% or more makes a big deal, as you will see later in this book.

He advised me to take the $1,500 and roll it into a Roth IRA.

He said I could contribute to it on a monthly basis once I settled into my career.

I learned a lot from him at this stage, when he introduced me to tax-deferred investments, compound interest, and the importance of setting money aside each month to grow in the market.

Being in love with research, and with a newfound motivation for money under my belt, I started digging through everything I could find.

Of course, I was angry at first that some of my hard-earned money digging holes had been set aside for retirement.

I was 18 years old, and the thought of retirement was so far off that I wanted to have the money right then and there.

The truth is it pained me to put the money into an investment vehicle like a Roth IRA at 18.

I thought of all the things I could have purchased.

But it was the best lesson I could have learned, and learning it firsthand was important, as well, since I may not have started my own personal retirement account without that hard summer of landscaping.

It was an unlikely lesson from digging holes.

Fast forward to my New Teacher Orientation in Maryland and a small presentation provided to us on our state pension.

The pension was one of the main reasons I chose to become a teacher.

It was never going to become a get-rich-quick scheme, but it would provide a slow, steady path to prosperity in the right district.

I also appreciated the security provided but knew it wouldn't be the answer to complete financial freedom.

I'll never forget the response I received to what I believed was an important question for someone starting out in any field.

When an older presenter came around I asked, "Do you have any information about other retirement options outside of the pension?"

The response might shock you, but she patted me on the shoulder and said, "You're young. You don't need to worry about that, yet."

This quick interaction bothered me a great deal.

I began to wonder how many other teachers were told not to seek out further investment opportunities.

I shudder to think what would have happened to my financial plan had I taken her word.

From what I had learned, the pension would not be enough for me to enjoy the retirement I had envisioned.

It has always been a strength of mine to see far into my own future, and I did not like the idea of waiting for pension income that would be taxed without any sort of supplemental money to afford me the life I envisioned.

And it seems year after year those that retire tell me it's going to be tighter than they anticipated.

Needing to work in retirement and *wanting* to work in retirement are two different things.

It became my mission to touch base with some established colleagues upon my first few months on the job.

Fortunately, for me, an unpopular decision to split from the faculty lounge where my team would eat everyday lead to a new friendship with a soon-to-retire ESOL teacher.

She was conscientious enough to ask me how I was planning for my future before I could even ask, so the meeting was fateful in many ways.

Within a week she had introduced me to her financial advisor, who - little did I know - represented a nationally-recognized, high-cost firm that provided 403(b) variable annuity products.

If you paid attention to the first section, you know this is not an ideal setup – at the start.

Upon our meeting, we discussed my desire to invest in a tax-deferred, 403(b) retirement plan, which my workplace endorsed.

I began setting aside $125 from every paycheck, or $250 a month, and felt amazing about my future prospects in terms of earnings.

Two years went by and a continued interest in personal finance had grown into a full-on obsession. Now I'm not a Certified Financial Planner ™, but I really devoured Money Magazine and Kiplinger's on a monthly basis, and started reading books on personal finance, stocks and investing.

I flew through works by Tony Robbins, Suze Orman, Dave Ramsey and more - even studying up on real estate with the likes of Bigger Pockets' Brandon Turner.

As I peeled back the layers of the financial world, I started to come across some very concerning facts.

What I would soon find out became the catalyst for writing this very book.

Fees Can Kill Your Retirement Plan

After a great deal of reading and research I got the courage to reach out to my financial advisor and ask how much I was being charged in fees for my actively managed portfolio.

The answer was 1.83%.

This may not sound like a lot at first, but this was just the fee for the active management.

Rolled into the annuity plan were a whole other litany of fees that were siphoning my total investment monies away from my future total.

And the more I learned the more I became nervous.

After some calculating, I learned that sticking with the plan could cost me over $300,000 in total fees and diverted funds over the course of my career.

These were fees I'd pay for them to try and beat the market and cover their costs in hiring advisors, paying taxes and marketing.

Because the plan was also a *variable* annuity, it would become a monthly check that would fluctuate with the markets on a month-to-month basis.

I'd never be able to rely on a consistent check each pay period.

Clearly, there was no way I was going to allow so much money to be lost, since the money forgiven would require me to work even longer in my current role.

In the grand scheme, $300,000 is a lot to the middle class.

I love what I do, but who wouldn't want the ability to retire a few years early?

It took me about a week to research and back-check all the 403(b) providers our district provided.

I found that Fidelity Investments was the only provider in my workplace plan that would allow me to take near total control of my investment account.

The move from the high-cost annuity provider with a fancy acronym to Fidelity would allow me to decrease my overall management fees from what were probably closer to 2.5% down to 0.05%.

There was to be a 5% surrender fee to move money out of the high-cost annuity and into the low-cost 403(b) with Fidelity.

I paid that fee, but it took some careful consideration.

There will be more on this move later; however, it's important to know two things if you're considering a move:

- How much will the surrender fee truly cost?
- How long will it take me to recover the money paid in surrender?

For me, the 5% surrender against my current balance was always going to be less than keeping my money in the high-cost annuity over the long haul.

What You Don't Know Can Hurt You

I had invested with the insurance/annuity firm for over two years by the time I made a change to my investments.

I know many of my colleagues have been investing with the very same firm for 15 years or more.

Here's the problem with fees: Over 70% of investors do not even think they are being charged at all.

Worse yet, most financial "advisors" are in fact brokers, which means their priority is to sell you into a product and receive a commission.

How are you supposed to get objective advice when the person sitting across from you stands to make a nice little bonus from signing you into their firm's financial products?

It's like asking your car salesman if you should buy a car.

Duh! Of course, you do!

Literally, what we do not understand regarding our finances and how firms structure their products is the reason why Wall Street has been able to siphon trillions of dollars from everyday Main Street workers like you and me.

In the years following my 403(b) rollover, I have worked to engage my closest friends in a discussion about the 403(b) plans offered at our workplace.

But it is tough to get people to open up about their personal finances.

We have been taught to trust our friend's recommendation or word of mouth from a neighbor, and to not to question anything after that.

We are also taught that finances are personal, so good information just doesn't get shared out in our circles.

Imagine they told us Derek's personal life was personal. We wouldn't be able to share his dirty secrets!

All joking aside, most of us willingly put more work into investigating a depreciating liability like a car, rather than an appreciating investment like real estate, mutual funds or ETFs.

Any one of us with some type of financial issue will generally brush it under the rug and hope for a better outcome, like a large market return, the lottery or a generational windfall.

Investing your money for your future is the single best move you can make outside of killing off your debts, so do not get discouraged.

Get ready to take action!

I have broken this book into six sections with the goal of flipping the script on how difficult it can be to access sound financial advice.

In our first section, **Laying the Foundation**, you will learn how to right your mind regarding money. The human brain is the most powerful asset we have, and if you are to be set on the road to financial success, we must start by putting ourselves in the right frame of mind for wealth.

Pillars of Financial Knowledge will catch you up on everything you might have missed while focusing on, well, living your life. These are the things the literal 'pillars' of the financial world want us to practice, but we most unfortunately do not.

In **Getting Ahead** I will help you enact some very powerful moves and realize the value of saving even $5 a day. Most of the philosophies discussed here are easily found in high quality personal finance books, or select blogs and social media posts, but I'll add more details to give you a better explanation for how these simple moves can benefit you.

Understanding the Industry will attempt to pull back the hood on the financial services industry and make you a better investor and money manager. You should leave this section as a smarter overall consumer, and while many remain trusting of the financial services industry you will learn to be skeptical and more precise regarding to whom you trust your money.

Once we've made it through the first three sections, you'll be ready to **Make Your Move**. This section will help you decide where to best put your hard-earned money, so that you can seek a more comfortable retirement.

Finally, **The Ultimate Plan** is a recipe for diversification and wealth attainment. This plan can create multiple layers of financial security for its users, and it is a conglomerate of some of the best financial advice out there.

The objective of this book will be to **expose the pitfalls of your own personal finances** and **provide direct, researched advice and knowledge** that can help you attain your retirement goals.

Thank you for joining me on this mission to take back what is rightly ours.

You will walk away from this experience a more informed investor, and inevitably you can create a brighter future by focusing on your own financial "wealth-being."

Earning your passport to $1 million starts now!

UNIT 2
LAYING THE FOUNDATION

Finding Your Why

If you are like me, you entered your profession in order to serve others.

In education, some say it's a calling while others say we're crazy.

Either way, whether you've been in your role for only a few years or for over 30 years, somewhere deep inside of your heart you have a burning passion to improve the lives of others – or at the very least yourself.

But when it comes to investing your hard-earned money, making others' lives better does not put the focus on you - the individual, the investor.

In this section, we need to work to put ourselves over others – if only in investments.

Remember the adage, you must love yourself before you can love another?

When we're investing, we have to learn to take care of ourselves, before we can take care of others.

Since we do not learn a great deal about personal finance in school, most of us end up learning how to manage money on our own or from the example of others.

More often than not, though, we entrust our money to others and hope they are doing what is best for us.

As you will soon read, we will find there are better options than just simply handing someone else the keys.

We must also learn not to take what is remaining after expenses and find a way to spend the extra money on things we enjoy - instead of investing.

Investing has to become the priority.

It's simple, shopping brings us joy while investing isn't immediately gratifying.

That's one of the many reasons 75% of America does not have access to investable assets.

It's the same reason we grab a burger over making ourselves a salad.

We know what's better for us, but we are also driven by consumption and material items, so we cannot entirely blame ourselves...yet.

I promise you the salad *can* taste better than the burger, in time.

So can investing feel better than spending.

The problem becomes that we often find ourselves in an endless loop of working during the week in order to make up for our spending on the weekends.

Life becomes a never-ending game of catch-up, and then we look up and learn we're five years away from retiring but do not have quite enough to live the way we most desire.

As Jari Roomer said, "Use the weekend to build the life you want, instead of trying to escape the life you have."

In order to start our financial planning makeover, we have to first establish a *why* for investing.

I am going to ask you to be selfish and put yourself first.

I work in a field that requires me to put others before myself.

Meetings are centered around improving academic and school performance and we often go home thinking about our students and how to make their instructional experience better.

We work to create work for others to work on while we grade work and create more work for others to work on while continuing to grade more work....

You get the idea.

It is hard for anyone, really, to turn inward and put ourselves first. But I need you to get there.

A lot can change in a month's time, so let's first commit to a month.

One month will turn into multiple months, a year into multiple years, and then a decade into multiple decades.

In the end, a 30-year career will go by in a flash. Just ask any happy retiree.

So at this early juncture, I encourage you to identify *your* specific, individual reason for investing, because when you invest you deliberately set aside money for your future.

What is that future for which you're investing?

Do you plan to pay off your mortgage and live a quiet, sustainable life away from all the hustle and bustle?

Are you excited to play golf multiple times a week and travel across the country a few times a year?

Maybe you are planning on selling your current home and settling down somewhere warmer in a brand-new build.

The key here again is to be selfish.

I dare you.

Write your why below.

I will invest in my financial future so I can…

_____.

If you develop a strong enough reason, you will make life altering financial corrections in the present, instead of waiting for some oft-handed future where you will – hopefully - have enough money.

If you decide to wait for more money before you start investing, you'll find something else to spend it on or stick your head in the sand and ignore reality.

There is no better time than now.

It is likely that if you are reading this book, you are already saving and/or investing some money, or at least planning on it.

Maybe you're just brushing up and seeing if your plan is missing anything important.

Or maybe you're a new hire that received this book in the hopes of growing a million-dollar account.

If you are going to get a good start, and begin enjoying - no, that wasn't a typo - the pinch of putting more money toward your future, you must have a strong enough **why**.

Why are you eating the salad instead of the burger?

Maybe you saw your parents struggle with money, and you want to distance yourself from that experience as much as feasibly possible?

Maybe you have rich tastes and want to establish a legacy?

I'm investing for my children and a kickass home with a writing table overlooking the pool and the ocean.

In reality, I want them to know their parents are financially set. See, I believe our children deserve the right to pursue their own personal and financial dreams, without the burden of their parents needing money or support.

A gift such as this only comes down to two things: **planning** and **action**.

First, I made this decision prior to my wife and I having children. I was 26 years old and had a long investment horizon.

Second, I have worked a number of side hustles to make sure these investments are on track.

My parents bestowed the very gift of financial freedom upon me and my brothers, even though they had to start from a much deeper hole.

I believed it would be a phenomenal gift to give our children the same security, and a terrible mistake to fail to provide this opportunity for a second consecutive generation.

They gave me such a great platform, and I knew it would be a shame to screw it up.

If I continue to stick to my plan and continue to increase my contributions with each and every raise, I should become a millionaire before the age of retirement.

If my returns are better than expected, I could become a multi-millionaire.

If this sounds too good to be true, I promise it's not.

As you will find later in this book, individuals earning much less than a teacher's salary have found their way to financial freedom, but only with a disciplined approach.

How did they do it?

Maybe they had a strong enough **why**.

Great authors on the topic of personal wealth attainment discuss setting goals and having a strong enough reason.

They talk about how our thoughts become our actions, and that we can change our financial destiny by expanding our vocabularies while using the law of attraction.

Writers such as Tony Robbins, the author of *Money: Master the Game* and *Unshakeable*, and Robert Kiyosaki, who wrote the most popular personal finance book to date: *Rich Dad; Poor Dad*, have empowered millions of people to change their stars.

You will find some of their teachings - along with others - sprinkled throughout the upcoming chapters.

We are all going to stand on the shoulders of giants.

I hope to empower everyone that goes along on this journey, so that you may seek greater clarity on this often-confounding area of our lives.

Someone once said if your dream doesn't make you cry, then it is not a dream at all.

So I encourage you to sit down and document your reasons for wealth attainment.

Ask yourself, "What kind of life do I want to have?" And "What are the behaviors that will get me there?"

Make sure it's something greater than "retire comfortably."

Just like my teaching philosophy, we must set out to put our goals far out but still within reach, so that we may overshoot the baseline that would make us successful.

Perspective is Everything

At this point you may already be having some lingering self-doubts.

He's going to become a millionaire from teaching?

Maybe he teaches in a better county or district and has some generational wealth from which he can live off of?

You might think, "I won't be that lucky."

If you're already running these thoughts around, Kiyosaki would call you out and say that you're "thinking poor."

In Kiyosaki's teachings, having a poor person's mindset can derail you from ever expanding your context of what is possible.

I encourage you to think it is possible, even if everything else in your life has told you it is not.

In my case, I was lucky enough to have my undergraduate education paid in full.

Once the amazingness that is science took hold of me during my senior year of college, I knew I had to tack on an extra year to work as a science teacher.

Prior to that, I majored in English and psychology.

The extra time required student loans on my part because my parents only committed to the four-year degree.

But I've never regretted the move for an instant.

Were my parents rich to be able to afford college for all three of us?

No, at least not at first.

My parents are the classic American high school love story that survived and even thrived.

My mother had my oldest brother when she was 16.

My dad, coming from a hardworking, six-child farming family, enlisted in the military and set his young family up on a new path.

Two years later, they had the middle brother and they worked their way up through military barracks and food stamps, finally settling down in Western New York.

It wasn't long after, having completed their degrees by going to night school and working varied shifts, they were on a new course for wealth.

Now in their 30s and with more income on a per-month basis, my mother pronounced she wanted one more child in the family.

That was me!

My brothers always told me I grew up when mom and dad had money, but they never did it in a way that made me feel bad about it.

When my parents got a hot tub and I was still living at home, my middle brother said, "Yeah, we had a hot tub too. He'd pee in the tub and I'd blow bubbles."

And, of course, the cutting the toes off the shoes so they would fit and all the hand-me-downs versus the new clothes I got.

What they lived through fueled them. It put their backs up against the wall, and they learned to climb too.

Fortunately for me, all four of my family members instilled perspective into my upbringing. They always shared stories with me and showed me pictures of their past.

We even traveled back to where my dad was stationed at a Strategic Air Command Base during the Cold War.

They'd show me the hangar he worked in and the officer's quarters, which no longer exist due to business development.

My dad would tell me about 2:00 AM alerts in the winter where they didn't know if it was a drill or if they were going off to war.

And my dad always shared the story of how my older brothers split a large pizza with their parents every Friday, when all they had after expenses was $10.

Meanwhile, over 25 years later, I went out with mom and dad to different restaurants every Friday and was able to order just about whatever I wanted.

Ironically, it was often pizza - a lovely cheese.

Kevin McAllister's favorite.

Their stories became a part of my fabric, and I made sure to honor my parents' hard work by contributing in various ways throughout the remainder of my teenage years under their roof.

I started working for my grandfather and uncle's produce farm at age 14, took my first job at Wegmans at age 16, and grunted that entire summer before college as a planter on a landscaping crew.

Throughout college, I spent summers working as a farmhand and tasting room server at a beautiful winery – Fox Run on Seneca Lake.

The perspective instilled in me really came to fruition in college, where I began finding ways to give back instead of solely earning for myself.

I became a resident assistant mainly to help my parents owe less in room fees, while I was able to earn $100 in stipend money every few weeks.

These things grounded me as a person, and the lives my parents lived continues to fuel my why.

I've been given a platform, and with that platform I can retire earlier than my parents even did, while providing my children the same or even better opportunities in life.

Maybe you know of a similar story or have benefited from someone in your lives.

Passing a financial legacy onto your heirs is a very powerful why, and it keeps me going in the right direction every day.

Some of you may have had to work your way through college, and that just means your story is even greater than my own.

Whatever you can key in on from your roots, make it a part of your fabric and work it into your why.

Your why is your purpose and with purpose we can accomplish so much more.

Okinawans ground themselves with their purpose every day, and Dan Buettner, CEO of Blue Zones - the study on centenarians - found that Okinawans may be adding up to seven years to their overall life spans - all by having a purpose.

Let's go get a better retirement to enjoy those seven extra years.

What do you say?

Setting Your Mindset

How do you handle stress and setbacks?

What is your ultimate view on failure?

These are important questions to answer in terms of redefining your reality.

Now that you have your why, we have to do one more thing before we get into the true financial moves that will begin to put you at the head of the pack.

Our ability to be successful and prosperous in life is directly related to how we think about the world around us.

A great observation made by James Allen states the following:

> "If circumstances had the power to bless or harm, they would bless and harm all men [and women] alike, but the fact the same circumstances will be alike good and bad to different souls proves that the good or bad is not in the circumstance, but only in the mind of him [or her] that encounters it."

He concludes it is necessary to stop complaining and feeling as if we are victims of circumstances around us, so that we can take control and be independent from what may have once caused us pain.

I listen to a lot of the conversations we have as professionals, and what I hear most is pain.

Maybe it's the way we like to communicate or find commonality, but a purpose grounded in pain is not what I want most for myself, nor my colleagues.

If we can gain control over ourselves and our minds, we can then feel empowered to take control of the world within which we live.

This can be quite motivating, but what actions can you take to start getting your mind on the right track?

Many great leaders profess to the powers of meditation and clearing one's mind.

Then and only then can they start to see the solutions.

Others find that working out and creating balance in their lives can have an astounding impact.

Suddenly, small wins in the weight room or running greater distances start to spill over into our confidence, which then spills over into your work and personal life.

One more set becomes one more accomplishment before a major deadline.

There is no doubt that everything we experience is a construct in our minds and its effect is determined by *how* we think of that experience.

Tony Robbins took an impoverished upbringing, made it a part of his fabric, and found that giving back while creating businesses that help people is a powerful formula for business success.

Now his businesses garner over $5 billion in revenue per year.

And, by the way, he owns an island and a resort in Fiji where he provides week-long courses in business and personal empowerment.

In a famous interaction with a fan, he mentioned that if his Mom had been exactly what he needed, he wouldn't have been as motivated to change his life and the lives of others.

For that he was thankful.

Instead of blaming her for a terrible start, he used it to elevate himself – taking James Allen's dynamic and proving that a terrible circumstance could not define his life.

Others are known to engage in week-long seclusion, separated from technology and the outside world in order to read and focus time and energy on discovering solutions.

The key here is that you have the power within you to change how you perceive stressful stimuli within your personal life and workplace.

I have found my workplace to be a consistent hotbed of complaining and negativity, where most of a teacher's stresses are displaced upon unruly classrooms, unsupportive administrators, and/or students.

It does not help that our school has performed at the lowest in our county for morale for a few years running.

It has required a great deal of discipline and persistence to come out on top of this, mentally.

When, in fact, if teachers had it within them to own their convictions to remain detached from negativity, then they might experience a greater connection to their core objectives in the profession.

Three essential courses help me to this very day, especially when it comes to stress, including: Educational Psychology, Child Development and Classroom Management.

It has always been my goal to teach for 30 years to gain the pension teachers are so fortunate to have; however, I knew I wouldn't complete the marathon if I became too stressed by the day-to-day work.

Those three classes helped me determine the following:

- What is age-appropriate behavior, and should I be stressed out by what these [in my case] 11-year-olds are doing?
- How do I design my classroom environment so that students are engaged and having fun, first, while underpinning everything with quality learning?
- How do I deploy the right amount of intermittent positive reinforcement to create a welcoming and redeeming classroom environment?
- Which type(s) of activities will create too much distress and destroy motivation, and which activities will create the right balance of eustress to motivate students to determine the unknown?

These are only a few of the key questions I was able to answer by taking the noted courses.

The answers have been indispensable.

According to a special report by Education Week, we know that 8% of young or early-career teachers leave the profession each year.

Would they fare better having these courses under the belt?

Many do stay for the long-term benefits and the joy they get from educating the students. And teachers often over-report their willingness to leave, without actually doing so. But if they finally do leave, the reasons center around stress, salaries, step freezes and childcare demands.

Those that work in tougher districts face even greater challenges, but as engineers of our environments we can work to manufacture a better reality.

The important difference in our next mindset alteration, which will be covered in "Getting Ahead: Paying Yourself First," is that we are aiming to gain something that is mentally empowering.

You have defined your why, now you will add a layer by making yourself bulletproof from negativity and stress.

Remember, destiny is not a matter of chance; it is a matter of choice.

We can either sit back and float powerlessly on the winds, or we can drive the ship and put the winds to use to get us to our chosen destination.

Financial stress can be one of the greatest headwinds of all, and we do not help ourselves by burying our problems or turning a blind eye.

In *Rich Dad, Poor Dad*, Robert Kiyosaki shares a viewpoint from his rich father.

In the book, the rich dad confides that every person at every level has problems with money.

Governments, corporations, small businesses, and employees of all types experience trouble.

His rich dad would go on to explain that the difference between the rich and the poor is that the rich discuss their financial issues with experts, in a manner to solve them as opposed to complaining about them.

They sit down at lunches and meetings and find resolutions so that they can improve upon their situations.

The rest of us succumb to **The Ostrich Effect**, where we bury our heads in the sand and ignore what's going on around us.

It's our defense mechanism.

Then, we wait for the next paltry raise if it comes at all.

Later, we will discuss ways to overcome financial struggles to put the chips on our side of the table.

No more sandy heads here.

For now, it will be important to gather all your intellectual power and motivation to rise above the stressors you have experienced thus far.

In an example of just how strong the mind can be, Robbins referenced a study that was done to see the effects of how people think about stress.

Specifically, the test tracked a subject's heart rate.

When an increase in heart rate was associated with negative thoughts, the participants released a stress hormone.

Others that believed their increase in heart rate was preparing them for something important did not release the stress hormone.

Quite literally, *how* we think about the world around us informs our thought processes and affects our internal body reactions.

Proving once again the connection between the mind and the body.

Professionals in any field cannot seek wealth unless they shake negative thoughts and schemata about the world within which they work.

The negative thoughts cloud our minds and distract us from life-altering conversations, like the one I had with my friend and ESOL teacher early in my career.

Had I stayed in the lounge listening to all the complaining, I might not have written this book.

I might not have retired wealthy.

Imagine that.

More importantly, we all must shake negative thoughts and doubt when it comes to ourselves and our money.

Let's remember, our self-worth is not defined by the numbers in our bank accounts.

It takes a lot of work to get our minds over our matter, but there's no better reason than to start now.

Think about the sources of negativity in your life. How can you act to cut them out so you can clear your mind and shift your focus?

What would you do with that extra time?

In what ways can you turn a negative into a positive, just as Tony Robbins did?

If you've made it this far then you must have a deep desire to change your mental construct.

This is a good thing!

And you must remember to have patience, because you are fighting hundreds of thousands of years of evolution that has prewired everything from what goes bump in the night to what's hiding behind that bush.

Now, we must raise our consciousness regarding money if we are to become masters of it.

The Law of Attraction

Is it true that you can envision $20,000 and bring it to life?

There are books and studies based on the law of attraction, and many who have put it to use swear by its powers.

Thoughts are seeds for action.

Plant a seed and it will grow.

- Jim Carrey made himself a $10 million check and carried it around with him everywhere he went. Sure enough, he eventually signed a $10 million contract for Dumb and Dumber. Now he's worth over $180 million.

- Jack Canfield, who wrote *Chicken Soup for the Soul*, imagined earning $20,000 and eventually he was offered a large advance on his first book. He is now worth $50 million.

- Dwayne Johnson, best known as "The Rock," had $7 in his pocket when he hit bottom and decided he would never be poor again. From that point on he got to work and has amassed over $400 million and counting, as he continues to build empires of reliable cash flowing businesses around himself.

On the flip side, some of us put a $1,000 iPhone in our minds and make that a reality.

Thought is powerful, and it is the same exact reason you have found a way to drive the car you've always wanted or wear that expensive Apple Watch you do not *truly* need.

Something about you desires something in the universe, and your thoughts influence the actions to make it reality.

Jack Canfield only envisioned $20,000, and eventually he received a $1 million check from his publisher and has received royalties from his books ever since.

Now, I'm not suggesting you go and envision a $5 million mansion with a heated pool and a view overlooking the most amazing ocean view.

That is terribly self-serving, but for some people it might be the most motivating vision.

And you could indeed get yourself there.

At this early stage of the book, it's best to envision a $1 to $2 million retirement portfolio.

It shouldn't go overlooked that many of the top motivators suggest dreaming big in order to create massive action.

Tony Robbins is a big proponent of dreaming big, because he would tell you the numbers you think you need are often quite within reach.

One example he provided in *Money: Master the Game*, involved a businessman that wanted to own a private jet.

He desired the freedom to travel wherever he wanted and to do so on his own whim.

Little did the guy know he'd have to put up anywhere from $3 million to $90 million for his own jet.

So Robbins suggested chartering a jet a few times a year, which would lower the amount he would need and help him avoid all of the maintenance costs.

Maybe you rent the $5 million home for a few days, instead.

Skip the mortgage, taxes and upkeep.

The law of attraction only works when you change your context and destroy your paradigms for what is real in life.

In fact, Robert Kiyosaki says the majority of people hold themselves back because they do not have the willpower to change their context.

Anyone who was able to think outside the box and change their context was able to change the world.

In *Retire Rich, Retire Young,* Kiyosaki describes how Henry Ford and the Wright Brothers had to have thoughts outside of their current context to bring their ideas to life.

The Wright brothers, Kiyosaki says, had to disregard the idea that humans cannot fly and find a safe place to test their plane, failing repeatedly in order to put humanity in the air.

Henry Ford had to envision a different form of locomotion and get away from animal-first forms of transportation.

These ideas were extraordinary for their time.

Each one of these exemplifies the power of changing one's context and putting the power of thought and the law of attraction to work.

In Earth science, we discuss how we are the universe's way of understanding itself.

Scientists have this perspective, because our bodies are made up of the remnants of stars, including: oxygen, carbon, hydrogen, calcium, nitrogen and phosphorus.

When it comes to examples like Henry Ford and the Wright brothers, is it safe to say we are a way for the universe to advance upon itself?

Technology has the ability to improve our lives and make it easier to conduct daily practices, while inevitably moving society forward in a profound way.

It's a powerful thing to realize that any technological advancement had to exist within the human mind, first, before it could become reality.

If our thoughts have this kind of power, how could we not envision greater wealth and comfort?

Maybe only then we will act in ways to get closer to that reality.

Using your mind, you have the power to create a new chapter in your life story, rewrite the script, and bring to life just about anything you dream up.

Our thoughts govern our actions, and if we think poor thoughts then we will act accordingly.

If we think negatively, we will act negatively and attract others that are negative too.

You already know misery loves company.

If we think richly, then rich actions will follow.

We will pursue endeavors that expand our context and generate income, such as reaching for a higher position, taking seminars to grow our side hustle into a full-fledged business, or checking out books from the library to expand our reality and grow individually - so that when opportunity finally does knock, we can kick down the door.

Now that we've put you in the right frame of mind for wealth, it's time to crush some paradigms that hold most of us back from obtaining wealth in the first place.

One million dollars.

Even if it's just a seed now, it can grow.

Congratulations on making it this far. Now, your financial education begins!

Get ready to join the 25% with investable assets but remember only you can determine how you earn your passport to wealth.

ADAM N. HEROD, M.ED.

UNIT 3
PILLARS OF FINANCIAL KNOWLEDGE

The Truth About Assets & Liabilities

The following section will be a crash course in key personal finance philosophies.

We will waste no time in getting right into it.

First, anyone on the path to personal financial well-being must understand the difference between an **asset** and a **liability**.

According to Robert Kiyosaki, an **asset** is simply something that puts money in your pocket and a **liability** is something that costs you money.

The age-old test of Kiyosaki's asset-liability philosophy is the greatest purchase of our lives: our home.

Most people believe their home to be an asset, since it appreciates and builds value over a long period of time.

Although your home appreciates in a good market, which means its value increases over time, it is technically taking money out of your income stream every month - money that could go toward other things like debt payoff, saving and investing.

On a positive note, paying your mortgage does become a forced storage for your money; however, it isn't something you can use right away, such as a paycheck, revenue from a rental or dividend income from an investment.

Therefore, when looking at a monthly statement your home falls into the category of liabilities.

So when is a home an asset, you might wonder?

Consider a rental property that earns you $300 a month after the mortgage, home insurance and utilities are paid.

An added $300 per month would fall into the category of assets.

If you were to own three income-producing properties earning you $300 per month, then you might be able to cover some of your living expenses, groceries and maybe more!

If this sounds interesting, I'll add more to this conversation at the end of the book, when we build our **Ultimate Plan**.

Let's return to the home being an asset in your long-term portfolio, however.

There is some truth to the idea that your home is a valuable tool in your path to wealth attainment; however, we must do the following in order for this to be the case:

- pay every mortgage bill on time
- own the home for at least 4-5 years to build equity
- realize appreciation or growth in value
- refrain from tapping the equity on the home to make renovations or make expensive purchases, lest we fall behind on payments and the bank reclaim our home
- sell at a higher value than what we purchased the home

But once again, in Robert Kiyosaki's view, if it is not putting money into our pocket on a daily, weekly or monthly basis, then it cannot be considered an asset on your monthly statement.

Assets are what the rich have a great deal of, including rental properties and businesses.

The glaringly simple difference between cash flow into our accounts and expenses can exacerbate an already muddled financial future; however, we find that many across America are adept at adding liabilities to their balance sheet, as opposed to assets.

Let's move to build assets.

Your Financial Picture

Your next task will be to create a clear financial picture for yourself, by tallying up all your assets, liabilities, income and expenses.

You can easily do so by filling out the following template or using an online net worth calculator such as the one found at Nerdwallet.com.

Completing the provided balance sheet can be the most revealing and motivating exercise.

Since we are at the start of this journey together, it will be important to know where you stand.

Do not worry if your numbers don't come out the way you would like.

Assets		Liabilities	
Total		Total	
Income		Expenses	
Net Worth			
Total Assets			
Total Liabilities			
Total Net Worth (Assets - Liabilities)			
Profit/Loss			
Total Income			
Total Expenses			
Total Profit/Loss (Income - Expenses)		Total	

Most of us are not aware of our own financial picture, and when it's finally revealed to us it can be a reason for us to create massive action.

So please do not shut down.

Now that you see whether your net worth is positive or negative, it can be a reason to dig deeper and move away from the mainstream of society keeping up with the Jonses.

It's Never Too Late

Change and improvement can occur at any point in your life.

Consider that Robert Kiyosaki is worth $100 million and he did not truly start his financial dominance until his late 30s.

Sara Blakely has a net worth of over $1 billion and started her empire at age 27 with only $5,000.

Colonel Sanders sold his first Kentucky Fried Chicken restaurant at age 65 and the company is now worth over $15 billion.

There is no right or wrong age to start turning the ship and depending on where you are in your financial life it may take a few miles to change course or a few hundred feet.

Either way, you likely already started when you picked up this book.

I often think it is helpful to work on your financial life as an athlete might.

Consider a professional athlete that is told he or she is weak in a particular area.

If the athlete wants to outperform an opponent, wouldn't the athlete work on that weak spot in order to shore up his or her game?

We should be no different!

If we think of our financial lives as athletes think of their bodies - identifying weak spots and strengthening them - we can better perform the exercises needed.

This kind of mindset can be helpful, instead of the one that gives us the unfounded "permission" to stick our heads in the sand and ignore everything around us.

Resist the urge to stick your head in the sand.

Ostriches, we are not.

If you truly need a palate cleanser, try adding up all the money you have ever earned, including tips and money from mowing lawns or other side jobs.

It won't be a perfect number but try to ballpark it.

In *Your Money or Your Life*, Joe Dominguez and Vicki Robin use this as one of their nine steps to gaining back control of your own personal finances.

It can be quite empowering to see just how much you have been able to put up.

Write it here: _____.

It's powerful to make it real and tangible, even if it's only on paper.

In their book, they find that most people have enough money to make them happy right now.

The problem lies in their consumerism and lifestyle, which people think is warranted by the hard work they do.

Then, once they've worked hard at a job they do not entirely love, they feel it's best to spend money on grand distractions, clothes and entertainment – especially on weekends.

The authors are right in challenging us to not use our hardworking jobs as an excuse to live outside of our means.

Instead, tap into a lifestyle change to cut back and enjoy the wealth benefits of our hard-earned dollars.

I'll take the mental repose that comes from having money in the bank over a new car or a closet full of new clothes.

The Truth About the Rich & the Wealthy

An accurate measure of wealth is what is in your heart.

Truthfully, the majority of us that do not have a great deal of money pine for it and imagine it will bring us great joy.

Money does talk, but Robbins would tell you that you already have everything you need in your life to feel happiness and wealth outside of money.

Really!

If you can see this, then you have already won.

Recently, Jim Carrey has been quoted as saying, "I think everybody should get rich and famous and do everything they ever dreamed of so they can see that it's not the answer."

It's about purpose and the goodness we feel from benefiting others.

We have it within us to feel great joy and happiness in the face of any adversity, and it is vital to our mental well-being that we do not gather our self-worth from our bank statements.

All of you reading this book make a positive impact on the planet, and without your contributions society would be in a much worse state.

You see, being wealthy can be having all of your family under one roof or being healthy enough to enjoy your favorite sports.

You want a real money shock?

If you make over $16,000 a year you are already wealthier than 60% of the planet.

You are wealthy.

When it comes to money, though, there is quite a difference between having a rich salary and being wealthy.

Now that we have established that you can feel wealthy and happy without money, what is the true definition of someone who has monetary wealth?

From all of my research, my definition of wealthy is the following:

A strong position of financial resources growing in various assets, savings and investment vehicles to create layers of protection against any negative financial events.

A Picture of Wealth

403(b):	$400,000
Roth IRA:	$200,000
Stocks:	$80,000
Emergency Savings:	$21,000
Regular Income:	$70,000 per year
Rental Income:	$600/month
Side-Hustle Income:	$1,000/month

When we analyze the above portfolio, we see different sources of income that are either taxed upon disbursement or not taxed.

We see different reservoirs of wealth that are either flowing cash in or growing capital.

We see different sources of income and layers of protection if a few bumps come along in the road.

Whereas an example of someone who is rich may have the subject earning $100,000 per year, but only from one source.

The earner has the income potential to be financially well-off but isn't because of the expenses he or she has.

See, you can have a rich salary and live paycheck to paycheck, and you can have a low to moderate salary and become wealthy.

Don't think everyone that makes six figures is wealthy.

It all comes down to how much you are able to put to use, and how much protection you have against downfalls.

Kiyosaki says wealth can be measured in time.

You could have $1 million, but if your expenses are $100,000 a month then you only have ten months.

Thomas J. Stanley, who wrote *The Millionaire Next Door*, stated the rich are generally income statement rich.

This means they have a hefty sum of money coming in on a monthly basis, but their end balance after expenses may be peanuts.

Many Americans fall into this category, considering that anywhere over $100,000 per year can be considered income statement rich.

Stanley found that many of the income statement rich were bogged down by numerous liabilities associated with the lifestyle they needed to convey.

Consider the lawyer with the Preserve Estate, fleet of vehicles and to-drool-over vacations.

He or she could be pulling in over $300,000 a year, but since the individual has so many lifestyle liabilities, they will fail to have wealth.

I recently read about someone who earns $800,000 in bonuses each year but finds it hard to live day-to-day.

"I simply don't make enough money," he said.

I always find it interesting that in desiring to talk to potential millionaires, Stanley found it difficult to locate wealthy families in what most would consider upper class, gated communities with multiple luxury vehicles parked outside.

Instead, he found the majority of millionaires living in smaller, single-family homes and townhouses with what seemed like everyday vehicles.

Interestingly enough, there were also many more millionaires who were married or had a significant other, rather than running it solo – a nod to finding that very special someone.

But, like you, I can already picture some of our acquaintances with the $600,000+ home, two large SUVs, a pool and yearly vacations.

Is it no surprise that many of them may actually be living paycheck to paycheck and have little to no accumulated wealth?

Lifestyle inflation turned their every raise into a new liability: a new car, boat, jet ski, bigger vacations and more.

One of my favorite conscience changing tricks – which can inevitably combat the lifestyle inflation that lurks behind your next raise - comes from *Your Money or Your Life*.

Dominguez and Robin challenge you to think of every purchase in terms of how many hours of your life it takes to buy that item you desire.

Typically, when we see a $300 jacket, we just see a $300 jacket.

Paying with $300 in cash might make us think a little bit more about the money we are spending, and if we pay with credit, we are less likely to even envision the $300 we are spending and borrowing against our future selves.

Instead, the authors suggest, think about the jacket in terms of your pay rate.

If you make $30 an hour that jacket will cost you 10 hours of your life.

Is the jacket worth 10 hours of your life?

Only you can decide that!

Dominguez and Robin found that no matter how much money people made they always thought they would be happier with more.

Really, what people in their study truly wanted was more time.

Ask those in their 80s and 90s what they recommend most, and they'll tell you to take that risk, live a life that is true to yourself, and work hard but don't be too busy to forget making a life.

Below, we're going to analyze the lifestyle behaviors of two hypothetical wage earners.

Let's say they earn $65,000 a year. After taxes, they bring home roughly $50,000 in cash.

We'll name them Mister Jones and Miss Penny. They'll earn the same stable rate of pay, but clearly their living choices have an immense impact on their income after expenses.

	Mister Jones	Miss Penny
Gross Income	$65,000 yr.	$65,000 yr.
Net Income (After Tax)	$50,000 yr.	$50,000 yr.
State Pension (7%)	$4,550 yr.	$4,550 yr.
Mortgage/Rental	$1,500 mo. / $18,000 yr.	$1,000 mo. / $12,000 yr.
Car Payment	$500 mo. / $6,000 yr.	$200 mo. / $2,400 yr.
Vacations	$3,000 yr.	$1,200 yr.
Golf Membership	$3,000 yr.	$0 yr.
Entertainment	$300 mo. / $3,600 yr.	$100 mo. / $1,200 yr.
Cleaners	$150 mo. / $1,800	$0 mo. / $0 yr.
Groceries	$300 mo. / $3,600 yr.	$300 mo. / $3,600 yr.
Clothes/Shoes	$250 mo. / $3,000 yr.	$150 mo. / $1,800
Frivolous Spending	$200 mo. / $2,400	$50 mo. / $600 yr.
Sum of Expenses	$44,400	$21,000
Income After Expenses and Pension Contribution	$1,100	$27,200

Mister Jones is caught up in the rat race, as can be exemplified by his spending habits.

He has an expensive vehicle that makes him look like he has money and spends $500 more per month on his housing when compared with Miss Penny.

Most of his overspending comes on the weekends, where he is more apt to order food out and spend money on entertainment.

Meanwhile, Miss Penny lives modestly, paying $500 less per month on her mortgage and $300 less per month on her car.

She understands that housing and transportation can be the two biggest expenses cutting into her financial freedom, so she starts there.

Notice she takes cost-effective vacations, does not pay for cleaners or golf, and has found ways to cut back on everything except for her grocery needs.

Now, you're probably looking at this and saying how in the world does she have $27,200 left and that she's not a realistic example of a $65,000 wage earner.

For the purpose of our quick example, I have left out property taxes, the cost of insurance, and other necessities, but let's say she has a grand total of $22,000 remaining.

What can her frugal lifestyle offer her?

$22,000 represents about 34% of her gross income. If she put half of that money, or $916 a month, into an investment vehicle that earns 7% interest she could have over $1 million by the end of her career.

If she put all $22,000, which would be quite a feat, she could end up with over $2 million.

What does Mr. Jones' lifestyle cost him?

Even if he could put all of his remaining $1,100 per year - or $91 a month - and earn 10% in returns he would only end up with just north of $100,000 after 30 years.

So are you of the wealth mindset or the spending mindset?

A quick way to test this out is to answer the following question:

What would you do with an extra $300 a month in a salary raise?

Those with a wealth mindset envision $300 more for cushion space in their budget, debt kill-off money or funds to invest and grow.

Anyone with a spending mindset jumps to a snap spending decision, envisioning a new car in their driveway, more nights out or more shopping trips each month.

The spenders will be the same individuals that complain about living paycheck to paycheck and not receiving enough in their raises - just like our $800,000 guy.

I laugh sometimes when I hear my 11 and 12-year-old students discussing brands.

In one of my final projects for the year, students are tasked with leaving Earth and colonizing an exoplanet outside of our solar system.

Inevitably, they end up bringing along with them Starbucks coffee shops, Chipotle restaurants and Apple stores.

The last time I checked, branded stores that sell food with a high markup were not required in establishing a new colony in another part of our galaxy.

Quite the opposite, really.

Yet these children reflect the decisions of their households in many ways, and it shows us just how much of our society is reliant upon the services provided by established franchises.

Meanwhile, there are millionaires all around you, but many of them are wearing jeans and t-shirts, splitting lunches and eating out at a rate of $40 for a table of two while driving Toyotas, Hyundai's and - at the most - BMWs.

Their spending habits are just different, according to Thomas J. Stanley.

These same millionaires get excited about assets and investments, while lowering their liabilities and paying only what they need in taxes.

Grant Cardone, entrepreneur and author of The 10x Rule, built a $5 billion real estate portfolio abstaining from wants.

He goes so far as to make sure every dollar in cash is plowed into an **asset** that brings him money.

He literally doesn't want it lying around without being put to work.

Those on a wealth path do not care if they *look* like money, because they know a few extra dollars spent chasing a brand only ends in heartache.

That's not to say they won't buy something nice for themselves, but if they are to spend the extra dollar, they will make it last.

One of my favorite wealth tricks is Jay Z's, "If you can't buy it twice, you can't afford it."

If something costs $250 to purchase, you are not allowed to buy it until you have $500.

I decided to take that to a whole other level and only purchase items when I could afford them five times over, which means I won't buy a $250 item on my wish list until I have $1,250.

Then $1,000 becomes my new "zero," where I won't allow the account to dip below $1,000.

The saving then continues and I further delay buying my wants.

One day, those numbers will be even higher.

Now, I'll admit learning and talking about money is not always exciting.

Waiting as long as I do to buy things is not always desirable.

Hence, You Only Live Once (YOLO), as my best friend will remind me when he pulls up in his new Jaguar F-Type.

ETFs, management fees, growth projections and markets are not for everyone, but sometimes we are the only ones we can trust, and it is more a necessity now than ever.

The COVID-19 pandemic showed us that.

One shoddy brick in our financial foundation centers around what I call the **Bucket-Spend Phenomenon**.

This is my phrase for explaining how we use our money, and it is rooted in how most of us were raised.

I remember getting $20 every so often from my grandmother. I'd put it in my wallet and I would think of the ways I wanted to spend that money.

Unfortunately, that money sits in dusty DVDs in a storage box somewhere.

Looking back, my whole goal was to fill my bucket – or wallet - with money and dump it all out to the things I wanted.

I'd hit zero and then be motivated to earn enough to get all that money back, but I can't say for sure I'd save it all and I know I was not an investor prior to age 18.

The 1% keep their money invested and growing and what they spend is a mere pittance of what they have in overall value.

This is what I call the **Pitcher Spending Phenomenon,** where our money remains in whichever container we choose, but only drips out in small increments from the valve.

The valve remains closed at all times and is only opened when we desire something, but that something will only represent a very small portion of what is contained within.

Choosing a pitcher for investing gives those dollars the power of RNA, or the ability to replicate.

And the pitchers denoted with names such as 403(b), 401(k), and Roth IRA do not sprout valves until retirement age, which forces our hands to remain in our pockets until retirement.

If we have a savings pitcher, we should control the flow from the valve but never fully pour it out.

And as long as we never bust the valve wide open, we will see our net worth grow and grow.

I'm broke: $80,000 in stocks. $1,500 in checking

That's not the kind of mindset we're often taught.

We know spending and managing money is truly a habit that has little oversight in our lives unless we make it so.

We do not have personal CFOs, so we must work to become our own system of checks and balances.

And just like we are quick to find excuses for not eating healthy or working out, we are quick to find excuses for our poor money habits.

The deck becomes stacked against us even further if we grew up in a house that had poorly managed finances.

From the day we recognize the value of money, we begin to construct our schemata around how to earn it and use it.

In order to change, we have to further study how the wealthy behave and think, and we're all a heck of a lot closer than we were before.

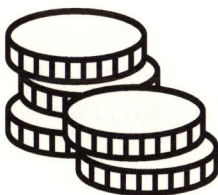

The Truth About Media & Financial Advice:

Truth:
If you reside in the United States,
you live in one of the highest
consuming nations on the planet.

Truth:
Businesses and marketing departments have
amazing budgets and psychological tools at their
disposal, which can all be deployed to get you to buy
their products.

Whether you agree with it or not, you live in one of the highest consumption countries in the world.

Seeing how most of us cannot come up with $400 for an emergency expense, we likely have room in our budgets to remove nice-to-haves and wants.

Could you give yourself a $100 raise each month, starting right now?

Print a PDF of your last credit card bill and see what you find!

Since we've covered our spending habits and budgets, we will now focus on where we can find reliable financial advice.

But just as we are phenomenal consumers, that also means our media sources operate under this premise as well and drive material that excites us and makes us consume more.

Financial advice is of course information, and it is capable of making us act in very reactive ways to the news of the day.

Oftentimes, people make financial decisions based on what is known as the **availability heuristic**.

This principle states that we are affected most by what we are consuming at that moment.

A fear of sharks or flying are perfect examples, because these are stories that are often covered by the media.

These stories make headlines because media outlets know they draw the viewer in, but most people do not know they are more likely to die from tilting a jammed vending machine than a shark bite in the ocean.

Once you know about the **availability heuristic**, you can use it to deflect the information that is presented to you on a daily basis.

For one year, I watched CNBC and trained myself not to fall for ads or make financial moves when talk shows highlighted specific moves to make or stocks to buy.

Sounds strange, right?

But think about this: those on a diet generally are still watching television and, inevitably, all the food and drink ads that come with relaxing on the couch.

It's tough, but they have to face that challenge in order to reach their ultimate goal.

Our mission: **$1 million**.

Unfortunately, we cannot search a new website without running into ads, and our email inboxes are filled up all the time, so I don't blame you if you are tired of deflecting everything that is thrown at you.

The pillars of the financial world know the average investor is at the media's very whim when it comes to financial advice.

It may very well be that most of us actually have the stomach to make it through drastic downturns in the market, but the rhetoric of news outlets and the conversations around us strike up fear and anxiety that can make us take inadvisable moves regarding our finances.

For example, had someone taken their money out of stocks at the pandemic bottom of March 2020, they would have missed out on a 75% recovery thereafter.

Since the pandemic bottom, we also know many people are holding onto much more cash and keeping their money out of stocks.

Market downturns are tumultuous and fast, and therefore most memorable, while market upswings are rewarding yet gradual.

The media doesn't help us with the onslaught of the **availability heuristic** and the rhetoric used.

To analyze this further, the general uptrend of the U.S. stock market- specific to the S&P 500 since its inception – is provided below. .

The graph shows the growth and progression from 1957 to 2018.

A Bigger Picture of the Stock Market

Standard & Poor's 500 performance since its launch in March 1957

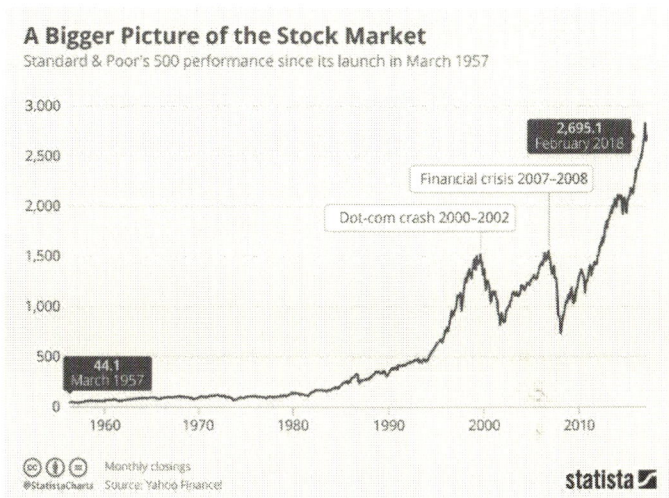

Figure 1 | Statista

Specifically, it is essential for us to train our eyes on the periods where the market retreated in the Dot com crash and financial crisis of 2007-2008.

What do you notice?

Although I'm sure it didn't feel like a short period of time for those experiencing layoffs and changing household demands, but the graph shows us the eventual relief that can come regarding the markets.

Specifically, the markets can bottom but have the chance to return to previous highs...

And most importantly even surpass previous highs.

Nobody is saying it is easy to hold out and keep your money in the market when it bottoms; however, history has shown that markets will recover, if only in due time.

John C. Bogle, the founder of the client-centered financial firm Vanguard, famously said that tracking changes in the market and watching big box networks can take away from the business of investing.

Why did he say this?

Bogle's investment philosophy attempts to remove all outside sources of distraction and human involvement in order to capitalize on the successes of multiple large businesses like those within the S&P 500.

Personally, he did not like all the banter for the everyday investor, because nobody at the news station - nor anywhere - could predict where the markets were headed in the near future.

Nobody.

We have to remember a media outlet's goal is to attract viewers and drive ratings, so if they can attract a crowd with flashy titles and economic banter that best suits the network, we have to take that into consideration when basing our own personal financial decisions on a network's suggestions.

Robbins analyzed this cycle in *Money: Master the Game*, with data from the third quarter of 2008, which marked the worst stage of the financial crisis.

During the worst of those times, people had pulled more money out than ever before, and the markets had lost more than $2 trillion in value.

When they sold their stocks at the bottom, they locked in unprecedented losses.

Princeton economist Burton Malkiel was quoted as saying,

> "We tend to put money into the market and take it out at exactly the wrong time. More money went into the market in the first quarter of 2000, which turned out to be the

top of the internet bubble, than ever before. Then by the third quarter of 2002, when the market was way down, the money came pouring out."

One of the all-time greats, Sir John Templeton, got his investing start in the Great Depression by buying up stocks that were crushed.

He is most famous for moving against the crowd, and instead of asking, "Where are the market opportunities?" for investment, he implores people to ask, "Where is the outlook most miserable?"

Because in that misery is an awareness of risk and - more importantly - opportunity.

For example, let's say you had invested $4,000 in Tesla around March 2020 when the stock was trading for $85 at the bottom of the COVID-19 crash.

When it climbed to $880 in January of 2021, you would have been sitting on over $41,000.

By April 3, 2020, Marriott hotels was trading around $59.

In March of the following year, it had surpassed previous highs to attain over $150.

A potentially safer bet on Marriott of $4,000 would have turned into over $10,000.

Personally, I like to envision buying stocks as ever inflating and deflating balloons.

Most will fluctuate in size depending on conditions, few will pop, and if all held together, they could take you up, up and away.

When Templeton made his money in the Great Depression, he bought 100 shares of each of the New York Stock Exchange companies.

At the time, they were all trading at or below $1- highly deflated balloons, but still intact.

As the market picked back up heading into World War II, his investments had grown many times over.

And when it comes to the general buying behaviors of the masses, Buffett tells us to be fearful when others are greedy, and greedy when others are fearful.

Just like red-tag sales at your favorite stores, we need to stuff our coffers full for emergencies and get rid of debts, so that when other opportunities come about, such as the next market downturn, we know we can weather the storm and maybe even buy some sales, as Sir John Templeton did.

Remember, we will be investing a set, specific amount of money each month into our retirement accounts.

Meanwhile, buying a dip on single stocks should only happen with 5% or less of our funds, and with money we know we can stomach losing if it potentially underperforms.

That's called market timing, and few ever succeed at that on a repeated basis.

Agents of Change

Those looking to rewrite their destiny regarding money subscribe to the teachings of authors, such as Suze Orman, Dave Ramsey, Robert Kiyosaki and Tony Robbins to name a few.

The ambitious and theoretical may seek out financial advice from PhD papers and investment kingpins such as Warren Buffet, John C. Bogle and hedge fund manager Ray Dalio.

These writers and investors have extensive knowledge and a track record of success in the personal financial and investing world.

Learning from them can give you some of the greatest insight possible into paving the road to prosperity.

They may not be as exciting to read as entertainment writers like Dan Brown or J.K. Rowling, but non-fiction books allow us to tap into the minds of those with experience.

Truthfully, though, we have to pan for gold in regard to the flowing river of financial advice that is out there.

Or follow **@themilliondollareducator** to have it done for you!

We have to train ourselves to decipher good knowledge from bad or trust the coaches and fee-only advisors out there to help us along the way.

As you know, there are numerous blogs and self-help books to choose from, but we must find what works best for us and make sure we minimize the amount of biased and marketed advice for financial products and services.

Remember, everything that is in a magazine is like a billboard.

Companies pay for real estate within the pages of those magazines, and not everything you read will be totally unbiased.

Also, a great deal of the changes we need to make can be made without purchasing services or seeking get rich schemes.

Anybody promoting a get-rich-quick scheme is likely marketing a product that is only going to make them richer.

There isn't a single person that can predict the movement of todays or tomorrow's market, as you now well know.

All one can do is diversify and hedge against market downturns by being balanced in their exposure – a.k.a. selecting stocks and/or funds from different sectors of the market - and remaining consistent in one's monthly investments.

Some of you might want to argue that Warren Buffett or John C. Bogle must have been able to predict the movement of the markets in order to become wealthy.

They've been wrong a few times, as any investor has; however, Buffett made his wealth by investing in valuable companies that were trading for less than what he thought they were valued and hardly selling.

John C. Bogle used index funds, low fees, time, and the productivity of hundreds of companies in unison to make his wealth.

There are various ways to bake bread, and each individual or home will require a slightly different recipe.

You can certainly set out to do it all on your own - and use this book to help you get your start - but remember that a third-party perspective without a conflict of interest can be a major benefit to you.

Again, reference 'fee-based financial advisor."

Now that we've erased some of your paradigms about money and wealth, it's time to make some subtle changes to your current income situation.

Getting Ahead will give you some fairly painless options to begin pulling the lever of change and swinging the momentum in your favor.

ADAM N. HEROD, M.ED.

UNIT 4
GETTING AHEAD

What's the Smart Money Move?

The more I read the more I see people struggling with the age-old dilemma:

Do I **(a) pay off my debts**, **(b) save** or **(c) invest my money?**

I cannot allow you to be the donkey that was stuck between drinking water or satiating his hunger, and never decided.

So the answer is simple...

All the above!

Before I get into my reasoning behind this, let's hear from some experts.

1. Mark Cuban.

Known for his often-outlandish persona around the basketball court and his endearing demeanor in the Shark Tank, Cuban has a great piece of advice when it comes to high interest debts - eradicate them!

Cuban notes that if you get rid of high interest credit card debt you will suddenly earn back 20%+ on your money, since you were likely paying over 20% in interest on the debt balance you owe.

2. Dave Ramsey.

Talk about getting to the point! Ramsey doesn't mix words when it comes to debt. His disdain for it is evident anywhere he speaks, and he even suggests bringing your emergency savings down to $1,000 in order to free yourself from debt payments.

Ramsey worked his way through college and has no love for car payments, student loans, and more. His approach condemns the societal debt norm we have created for ourselves and wants to rid us of the debt disease for good!

3. David Bach.

Known best for his book, *The Latte Factor*, Bach suggests paying yourself first and then taking any extra money you may have - say half of what you paid yourself - and devoting that to erasing debt.

His is a two-headed approach, where you're saving and killing off debts at the same time.

I have always believed in a three-headed approach for finances, and here are the core basics of each by priority:

- **Killing Debt.** With the wrong kind of debt in our portfolio (i.e., credit card debt and vehicle loans) our financial plans are weighed down. Make sure you're meeting the minimum payments on all of your loans and debts and never miss a payment.

- **Investing:** It is likely your workplace offers some type of retirement program. Start with at least the minimum percentage to receive an employer match – if you get one - and then commit to a 1-2% increase every year until you get to 15%+ in your 401(k), 403(b) or 457(b). Be a long investor, which means you will look to reap the long-term benefits of the growth in stocks, regardless of dips, as graphed earlier.

- **Saving:** By saving money early it allows you to build a cushion for yourself and your family. Professional advisors recommend anywhere from 3-9 months of emergency savings to cover expenses, so I shoot for the higher end in order to rest easy. The COVID-19 pandemic taught us the value of being on the higher end of the emergency savings spectrum.

You are probably asking yourself, "How do I save, invest and kill debt all at the same time?"

We have to sacrifice while we are young to enjoy financial freedom later.

Remember, even a little bit is better than nothing.

You must sit down and crunch the numbers to see if you are meeting your debt obligations, first.

There is no need to pay credit card interest if you have the money lying around, so make ridding bad debt your priority and invest the rest.

To Do:
Pay off all debts utilizing the debt snowball method, starting now.

and at the same time…

Invest enough in your retirement to receive the company match or be somewhere close to 5% of your income, starting out.

How might you implement this three-pronged attack?

Let's start with the **debt snowball method.** It is one of the best out there, and it has a built-in secondary benefit in giving us the positive feedback we need to keep the train rolling.

The snowball method has you rank your lowest monthly debt balances to your highest monthly debt balances.

You meet all the monthly minimums for every loan in your name but throw any extra cash you have at your lowest overall balance.

Once the lowest balance is paid off, you take the minimum payment and any extra money you were putting on top of that payment and apply all of it to the monthly minimum of your next highest debt.

Essentially, you accelerate the rate at which you're biting chunks of debt off your balance sheet.

With this method, we also capitalize on the feeling of winning and conquering our debts as we pay off each balance and roll the money over to knock down our debt burdens repeatedly until we're #debtfree!

Once all of your debt obligations are met, it's time to get your employer match - if you have one - and sock some money away on the side.

The goal is to take advantage of time and compounding when investing.

The recipe and the demands to make the three-pronged attack are going to be different for everyone, but if you go about it right the debt phase will not last forever.

This period of our lives is not easy.

You will feel stretched thin and exhausted most days, but this grind can have a very small window of 1-5 years if you do it right.

Remember, if the government started charging you $30 more per paycheck in taxes, you would have the money.

Sometimes we just need to put our backs up against the wall a bit and start somewhere.

By being smart here, my hope is that you will not be going out and creating more debts in buying material things as your cash flow begins to grow.

The reason I love the three-pronged attack is due to compound interest.

Compounding, which Einstein dubbed the eighth wonder of the world, is an important factor in our personal financial plan.

And all we need to do is start and use time!

It is widely noted Einstein said, himself, "He who understands it, earns it. He who doesn't, pays it."

In short, compounding is a force of nature.

To put this on display, let's analyze Ben Franklin's little-known story regarding his estate plan, which will attest to the power of the compounding philosophy.

One year, before Benjamin Franklin died, he made an addendum to his will to give the cities of Boston and Philadelphia 1000 pounds of sterling, or $4,000 in USD.

He included instructions that required the money to remain untouched, compounding for approximately 100 years.

A portion of the funds would be used by each city for special projects, and then the remaining would continue to compound for another 100 years.

Fast forward an entire century and the cities had at their disposal $6.5 million.

This was quite a vision from Mr. Franklin, and a great example for us regarding the power of compound interest.

A $4,000 U.S. dollar equivalent in sterling had turned into $6.5 million - all thanks to time and compounding.

The secret to compounding is that it requires you to set aside money in an investment for a good portion of time and leave it untouched.

30 years is the idea, but 20 is possible if you can commit more money to the plan.

As opposed to Franklin, who did not add any more money or request that new money be added, we will contribute to our accounts along the way.

Only with the power of compounding can $200,000 set aside little by little from all of your paychecks over the course of 30 years have a chance at $1 million.

I'd trade $200,000 for $1,000,000 every lifetime.

And see, that's where most of us go wrong.

We think we have to save $1 million outright, like our bucket-spend phenomenon, but with compounding we can *invest* a certain amount and earn more on top through the markets.

Just like Ben Franklin did.

Let's see a simplified example of the three-pronged attack, with someone who has a small amount of wiggle room in their budget.

Monthly Income:	**$2,400**
Rent or Mortgage:	$1,000
Food, Electric/Gas, Entertainment:	$800
Savings, Investments & Debt Repayment	$600

Let's say our subject can put up $600 a week of income after taxes.

That will bring the earner up to $2,400 a month.

If he or she needs $1,000 for rent or mortgage, and $800 for food, electricity, gas and some personal entertainment, that will leave our hypothetical subject $600 a month for saving, investing and debt repayment.

Let's say there is a student debt repayment of $250 a month, and a car payment of $150 a month - that leaves $200 for saving and investing.

What can someone do with $200?

Imagine our subject put $75 a month into a high interest online savings account that earns over 2% per year – which did exist pre-COVID - to protect from inflation, and the other $125 a month into retirement.

$125 per month invested into a pre-tax retirement account like a 401(k) or 403(b) can turn into the following over 30 years:

- $141,691 at 7% interest
- $246,741 at 10% interest
- $361,999 at 12% interest

These numbers don't sound like a lot, at first - and they sure aren't enough money to completely retire on - but it is a great foundation and these numbers beat the retirement totals for the majority of Americans today.

You are about to separate yourself from the majority of Americans, all from simply getting your start.

Not too bad for an investment of $125 per month.

Remember that if you cannot commit as much money now, you can always increase your contributions later when you have more wiggle room from your debt payoff and potential raises.

Don't forget, once your emergency savings goals are met you can take the extra money and roll it right into other buckets

The secret is that the sooner you start, the less you have to commit on a monthly basis.

And, remember, if you are smart your debt will not last forever.

You can seek side jobs and higher income opportunities to grow from your foundation of $125 to get to $250 or even $400 or more per month.

The power of time and compounding is interesting.

So what happens if you started this $125 a month at age 20, never increased the total amount of your investment and stopped at age 65?

At a 10% return your money grows to over $1 million, showing that just about anyone in the middle class can retire a millionaire.

You're liking this book if you're sitting there reading this in your early 20s.

If you're older, stay with me.

You'll find what you're looking for soon enough.

$1 million from $125 a month is possible?

That's two or three dinners out, where you instead stay in and cook or split a pizza with some friends.

What if you don't have $125 extra to spare each month?

Find it.

Create it!

That's a little over $30 extra dollars a week.

The opportunities we have to make money in the 21st century are boundless, and if you have a particular skill, like teaching or you are bilingual, you will see how you can put this to use in the subsequent chapters.

Remember that when saving, we're putting money aside for new tires or the breakdown of an appliance, and $1,000 may be enough to let you rest easier at night.

When investing, we're putting money toward our future and taking advantage of compound interest, which only helps our money grow beyond a low return savings account and beats inflation.

And when killing debt, we are freeing ourselves from the burdens of student loans, credit cards and inadvisable personal loans.

If you're looking at this and wondering if you can even stretch it to two of the financial initiatives noted, it will be smart to prioritize your debt repayments, first, and investing, second.

Ramsey would say to go all in on your debts, but as you saw earlier the power of compounding even $125 a month could get you to millionaire status if you start early.

This is an important area of focus because we can always find a reason to put off investing, and if you don't start getting used to the pinch early on you might get too comfortable and never start at all.

It's like increasing your fruit and salad intake earlier in life - it might not be sexy, but the outcome will be a heck of a lot better.

To Do:
Start investing right now.

What are the consequences of waiting?

Let's look at how much we would have to save from each paycheck to reach $1 million by age 65.

We'll compare different starting ages and assume a market return of 10%, which is a generous amount.

Age of First Investment	Amount Per Paycheck	Total Principal by age 65
25 Years old	$80	$1,000,000
35 Years old	$222	$1,000,000
45 Years old	$660	$1,000,000
55 Years old	$2,450	$1,000,000

Here's what's crazy about compound interest; the 25-year-old investing $80 per paycheck – or $160 per month

- does not necessarily need to increase his or her investment amount to reach $1,000,000 by age 65.

This is a lesson in taking advantage of time and consistency.

I'd rather feel the pinch of $80 early on in my career than the absolute chomp of over $600 per paycheck at age 45, all because I waited too long.

We must not forget our financial demands become greater in our 40s as our families grow, so starting early can only benefit us as our demands increase.

I Started Investing Too Late! Now What?

Every situation is different, so if you're late to the game try to take advantage of catch-up contributions, which can be made once you've reached age 50 and older.

Those old enough can make contributions on top of typical limits for 401(k)s, 403(b)s and Roth IRAs, which helps the investor catch back up to the growth curve.

In 2022, those eligible for catch-up contributions were able to add another $6,500 per year to their workplace retirement accounts, but even less in IRAs.

Fund Type	Allowable Catch-Up Contributions
401(k)	$6,500 per year
403(b)	$6,500 per year
457(b)	$6,500 per year
Roth IRA	$1,000 per year
IRA	$1,000 per year

Compound Interest

Let's look at a quick example of compound interest, which is known by many investors to be a powerful factor in generating wealth.

We're going to pretend that two people sit down and divvy up a deck of cards until each has 20 cards in their hand.

Their first bet is for 25 cents. Whichever card is highest wins the round.

25 cents doesn't sound like much, but by round eleven did you calculate what they're playing for?

$256!

By round sixteen they're at $8,192.

And for their last hand there will be $131,072 on the line.

"Well that escalated quickly." – Ron Burgundy.

Our investments work very much the same way, where we initially feel like we are looking at peanuts but later on everything looks intriguing.

Admittedly, it can be a little demoralizing when we look at our accounts and see so little early on; however, with the power of compounding our numbers can grow exponentially.

Compound Interest on $250/mo. at 10% Annual Growth

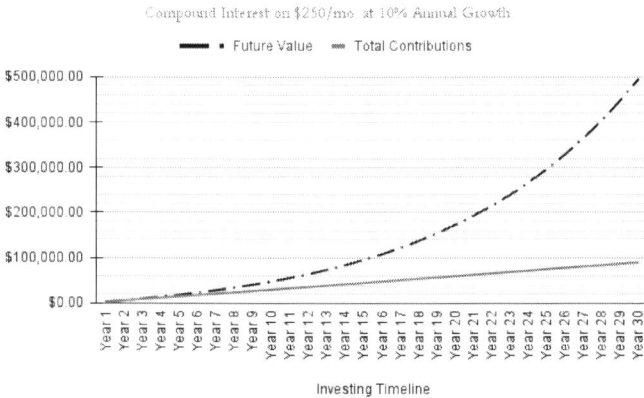

Investing Timeline

In the early years, we may only be looking at an account with $15,000 to $20,000 in it, and we'll wonder how we will ever have enough to retire.

But if we consider the power of compounding and invest and hold our money for a longer period of time - maybe working an extra five years - compounding can make our accounts grow beyond original expectations.

In the graph above, you can see by year ten the investor has about $40,000 *total*, which doesn't feel like a lot after ten years.

But by year 32, the investor's account is increasing by nearly $40,000 *per year*.

Start, even if it's small.

Again, time and consistency.

Let the metronome click away.

Paying Yourself First

It is a powerful thing to realize that within your paycheck, and, consequently, within your budget you have the means to make more money.

All without picking up a second job.

Let's start with David Bach's $5 latte example.

In this example, a woman had proclaimed to Bach she was unable to become wealthy through investing.

As Bach dug deeper, he found she was spending over $11 a day on breakfast and lunch items.

He challenged her to remove the morning latte and save $5 a day, or a total of $150 every month.

If she instead placed her money into an investment fund for 30 years, her $5 a day latte would turn into over $170,000 if it earned 7% interest.

At 12% interest, it would become over $430,00.

Bach's Latte Effect	7% Return	12% Return
Investing $5 per day for 30 years	$170,000	$430,000
Investing $10 per day for 30 years	$340,000	$860,000

*Figures do not take into account potential investment fees, which can range from 0.015% and higher

Remove her lunch habits and invest $10 a day, or $300 every month, and it would grow to over $340,000 and $860,000, respectively.

Cutting your coffee expenditures is often viewed as an essential move to becoming wealthy, but as we will find it is only the very beginning of your smart money decisions.

In fact, answering the question, "How can I make more money now?" can often lead to more exciting answers than the restricting inquiry of, "How do I cut back?"

In this book, we will not only become wealthy by cutting back and saving on the front end, but we will grow our personal financial wealth by expanding our work efforts on the back end.

To Do: Start an automatic deduction into a high yield, online savings account with a separate bank to build an emergency savings or an automatic contribution into an investment account.

It is a small feat to save $5 or $10 every day, but as you can see it can have a profound impact over time.

So how do you get started?

Automatic deductions.

You see, we need to beat the human psyche - the one wired for immediate satisfaction.

Plenty of studies have shown that if we have an extra $25, we're more likely to spend it than save it.

By simply paying yourself first - and putting the money directly into your savings or investment account - you are working against that little demon spender on your shoulder.

I don't want you to have the money burning a hole in your pocket, so it will be set aside before you can even see it or lose it to a wave of over-sweetened calories at your local coffee shop.

Better yet, set up an account with an entirely different bank so you can't access the money as easily.

This will ensure you don't derail your goals for sugar.

The harder you make it to access, the less likely you are to use it for things you don't truly *need*.

In starting with automatic deductions, you are making your first professional move toward your smarter financial life.

If you haven't put this book down for a minute to set up your first automatic deduction, I give you permission to do just that.

Start with whatever you can and aim for each deduction to occur bi-weekly on the same day as your paycheck.

Let's work together in this brief moment to start you off on a new path.

Why don't more of us use this simple strategy?

Frankly, there are two reasons we don't start off small.

1. We don't like restricting ourselves when it comes to our spending and indulging
2. And we focus a great deal on the short term and fail to plan for the long term.

When it comes to our financial futures, we have blurry vision.

In school, we are taught to understand history and learn from the past, but there are few opportunities to calculate and foresee what lies ahead in terms of our personal finances.

The future also fails to be tangible to us.

We're often afraid of what is to come, because we just simply do not want to think of ourselves as older and mortal.

Therefore, many of us put off our estate planning and advanced healthcare directives.

More **Ostrich Effect**.

But that doesn't give us the right to put things off when it comes to our savings and/or investments, lest we miss the amazing growth opportunities compound interest can provide us.

We started off with the "Latte Factor" because it's the easiest change we can make.

It does not require us to sign up for another job and spend time away from our families, and with a little ingenuity you can enjoy an even fresher cup right in your home.

To make significant changes, we will need to go much farther than cutting out a simple drink or two.

So let's keep rolling.

Cutting Back

In 2019, Bloomberg reported that over 40% of Americans admitted they would not be able to come up with $400 in emergency funds.

This is extremely concerning, as the rise of social media has persuaded an ever-consistent stream of people to succumb to lifestyle inflation.

When we see our friends traveling, buying new cars and new purses and having lavish dinners, we in turn view our lives through that scope and desire the same or better.

Remember, nobody is posting their failures.

Social scientists agree that there has never been a time where societal pressures have impacted us more.

Our access to social media feeds like Facebook and Instagram could be our own downfall and it may all be happening subconsciously.

Already, on our own and without the influence of social media, we begin to live more and more lavish lives when we earn more money.

We see a $200 margin and say, "Oh, now I can afford a _____."

This is the definition of **lifestyle inflation**, where our spending habits grow with our salaries.

Inevitably, we are unable to create any financial margin.

To Do: Create and increase your financial margin, year over year.

Financial Margin is a term that describes a stockpile of monetary resources that allows us to have financial confidence in the face of life's surprises.

Remember when The Rock had $7 in his pocket?

His financial margin was, well, $7.

It's a heck of a lot more now and it didn't happen by chance.

In his words, he got there by using his own two $%&@'d up calloused hands.

In America, we have a resounding tendency to desire fancy things, and we will go as far as owning those fancy things to appear wealthy, when in fact most do not have the cash - or financial margin - in hand to back their expensive purchases.

Most are borrowing against their future earnings, stretching themselves evermore.

So instead, we sit beneath a mountain of student and lifestyle debt and continuously fall to the rear on the journey to financial freedom.

Are you at-the-ready to tell someone you *had* to accumulate loans?

Dave Ramsey would call you out and say you did not have to, especially since he worked to pay his way through school.

You can't tell him any different since he paid his way.

Are you working hard to keep up with your monthly car payment?

I don't know about you, but I'd rather have the headache of getting into a standard $20,000 or less vehicle before buying a luxury vehicle I can't fully afford – requiring me to chase payments every month.

In his review of millionaires, Thomas J. Stanley, PhD found out most lived below their means and only bought large homes when they could more than afford the expense.

Back to Jay-Z's principle.

As an example, Stanley found that home expenditures for millionaires rarely eclipsed 25% of their **gross monthly income**, or the total amount they earned before taxes and expenses.

Are you living below your means, or did you jump up into a larger home too quickly?

How to Calculate the Cost of
Your Mortgage Against Your Net Earnings

Total Monthly Mortgage Cost $\div$
Net Monthly Income (after taxes, investments and expenses)
$= X$

$X \quad x \quad 100 \quad = \quad \underline{\hspace{3cm}} \, \%$

Ex. $\$1,000 \div \$3,900 = 0.2564$

$0.2564 \quad x \quad 100 = 25.64\%$

Use the above equation to figure out where you stand.

Remember **net income** is the money you receive in your bank account after taxes and any pre-tax investments.

I prefer the **net** figure amount after taxes and expenses, as opposed to the **gross** amount used in Stanley's book.

Thinking this way creates yet another layer of protection for our finances by protecting our ability to invest on the front end and live below our means regarding what's left over, after investing.

The net figure requires us to prioritize other items like investing, first, in order to keep the total housing cost at 25% or less of our take-home, or net, pay.

I get it. Many people will say your living needs to be prioritized, first; however, if we understand housing amounts to be the greatest expenditure of our lives then maybe we can handle a few fewer square feet in order to meet our immediate goals of freeing up our cash flow.

If you landed anywhere near 25% of your net income in the earlier calculation, then you are living more like a millionaire.

If you found out your home is consuming 30% or more of your income after taxes, you might be scratching your head wondering if you are in too deep.

And the picture as to why you may not have been able to invest as much is becoming clearer.

Choosing to live in a home that consumes more than 25% of your net income does not mean you won't become wealthy, but it does mean you have to be smarter about your other expenses in life and even craftier with your side-hustles to generate more income.

Can you make a move to live in a smaller home with a lower overall monthly mortgage?

Admittedly, this decision is much harder than giving up a $5 latte, but it's the fastest way you can work toward having greater financial margin, since our mortgage is one of the greatest expenses in our lives.

In fact, deciding which home to live in can be one of the single determining factors in determining whether you are wealthy or not.

Earning More with Multiple Streams of Income

For most of us, tackling how to save more money is the first move and it is the one that is most supported in our consumer-based society; however, we cannot forget that in America, we can make ourselves into anything we desire.

Creating greater financial margin can be a two-fold attack with saving *and* the accrual of funds from hustling your tail off.

With those two in action, a $5 splurge won't hurt as bad, especially, when you're up $90 for that week.

Notice I didn't say *if* you'll be up for the week, but *when.*

Never borrow against future income, which just leaves you chasing once again.

Pitbull said it wisely, "If you chase money, it'll run!"

See, the backbone of America – our middle class - applauds hours and time spent working.

It is a part of our fiber.

And although young people don't have the reputation for hard work, some of us have absolutely no choice if we are to make it - or make it out.

But at some point, when we've put in the amount of time to become the practitioners we are – regardless of the career - we have to capitalize on the rate we can demand in the market.

To Do:
Start a side-hustle to replace the amount of money you've committed to your retirement.

Maybe you are bi-lingual or you're an engineer and you're great at making mathematics relatable.

Maybe you crushed your ACTs, SATs or GMAT.

You have something the market needs.

Think of how many students struggle in reading and mathematics, or how many parents want their children to learn coding.

Although not every family can afford private tutoring services, there are a number that can, and furthermore desire to have their students excel for the prospect of exceptional secondary school opportunities.

Canned, center-based tutoring services work for a segment of our population, but some students need more direct curriculum support, which is where you can fill that void.

Parents will often pay more for direct, curriculum-based instruction from a seasoned professional.

This is where you can increase your rate while decreasing the overall hours worked.

Your goal should be to replace the monthly investment amount you just started.

So if you're committing $200 per month to your retirement, you might try to tutor one student for $50 per week, adding up to $200 in extra revenue per month.

Remember, multiple streams of income will always be the goal here.

Don't quit your day job, although some have built up enough business to do so.

Kevin O'Leary, aptly named Mr. Wonderful on Shark Tank, says, "A salary is the drug they give you to forget your dreams."

So early in your career, you might get excited for the 2-5% wage increases you might receive after each negotiation period.

But in starting your tutoring work, you might realize you could make $1,000 to $2,000 or more in a matter of one to three months, or less!

Why wait an entire year for a salary bump that may or may not come due to negotiations breaking down, market conditions, a global pandemic or more?

If you're not sure where to get started, tell some of your close contacts or friends you're thinking about tutoring and see if they'd recommend your services.

Elementary reading and mathematics are not terribly difficult to master, and the 1:1 ratio of curriculum-specific learning is often better for overall growth than the canned, one-size-fits-all services provided by larger tutoring companies.

The power of word of mouth and your attention to providing people a good service will be indispensable to you and your side-hustle.

Apps and services such as Nextdoor and Facebook only help expand your services, and you'll be up and running in no time.

Don't spend a lick on marketing. Start by talking to people you've already served – those that know the quality product you put out in the classroom.

Not interested in starting a tutoring service? Post-pandemic, employees are finding a wealth of value in the job market and have increased their salaries 25% or more simply by shopping their resumes.

It rarely hurts to try!

Getting Ahead by Never Falling Behind

If you have to borrow money for something you want, then you never had the money in the first place.

This is what I despise about services like Affirm, which allow you to pay over a lengthened period of time for items you cannot entirely buy in full, now.

By owing others, we continuously take money from our future selves.

It's easy to push our burdens off for the future, but to me - and others who hate debts - it creates restlessness.

Loans are designed to lure you into falling prey to our basic need for quick satisfaction.

Institutions offer a monthly payment that looks digestible, but their main goal is not the monthly payment – it's the interest rate they can charge you on the total purchase.

Financing is where they make their money, and most often provide in-house financing to control the levers of cash flow.

I love those little pamphlets from the auto dealers that say, "We can lower your payment," as they flash a newer model of our very own car and get me thinking about lower monthly payments and a newer model vehicle.

"Yeah, you know what a lower monthly payment looks like? How about zero, when I pay off this loan!"

To Do:
Stop taking out loans.

Are there any loans that make sense, though?

For the most part the answer is no, but Warren Buffett does believe in the home loan.

He thinks buying a home in cash is silly when that money might be able to grow 10% or more in the stock market.

Typically, real estate tends to grow 3-7% across a typical year, so even he did not buy his home in cash.

Instead, he put the money to work in the market.

What a simple, yet interesting way to think about money.

Another feather in the cap for investing.

I understand a recency bias due to unbelievable returns in the housing market will act to counter the above position; however, it's not always likely that someone will "earn" more through home price appreciation than their day job – as many did during the ramp up in home values during the pandemic.

A Note on New Vehicle Purchases

You might think of me as a miserable Scrooge after reading this section, but I find it difficult to be happy for those purchasing and posting about their new vehicles.

"You are just jealous," you might think.

But look at it from another angle.

Vehicles rarely gain value over time, except for certain collectibles, so most of us will not likely own a vehicle that appreciates in value.

And financing offices are offering longer payback periods to capitalize on interest charged to the loans, while offering what look like lower monthly payments.

So the sticker tag might say $35,000, but the overall cost of paying the loan on a $35,000 car at even a 3.0% rate for six years is over $38,000.

What's the monthly payment?

Try $530 a month.

Then, remember that you are now out a total of $38,000.

Had that same person invested $530 a month over six years and earned an 8% return rate he or she would have almost $50,000 to play with.

Take that $50,000 one step further and throw it into a low-cost fund for 20 years and even with no further contributions it could become almost $250,000.

But, again, we are not wired to think this way.

Now imagine sitting on the extra cash you have and when vehicles decrease in overall value across the market, you jump in and buy.

Talk about a life-hack!

Leases also rarely work, numbers wise.

Meanwhile, if you are able to own a vehicle for a longer period of time you'll have the benefit of restoring those monthly $200+ payments.

See, most do not like the judgment - or perceived judgment - that comes with stepping out of a cheaper or older vehicle.

The **invisible audience** may direct more of people's thought processes than we think, even though most of us grow out of this mindset by eighth grade.

Consumption, grandeur, and a need for relevance keep us in a cycle that makes others rich, not ourselves.

Gary Vaynerchuk, also known as Gary V online, is a Belarusian-American entrepreneur with a great message on social media.

If you need a punch in the gut or some inspiration, go find some of his stuff.

He delivers things that are to the heart of individuals and society as a whole, and one of my favorite quotes from him is as follows:

"...people end up buying cars and houses and clothes that they can't afford to impress people they don't like... [this] is the great epidemic in our society."

The pressure to be something and have material things in America is real.

It is reinforced all the time, and we often measure others by what they have.

I used to deal with this after I downgraded from my BMW 3 Series to a Toyota Corolla.

I remember a group of my students yelling out, "Nice car, Mr. Herod!" as they joked about the Corolla.

My response?

I did not say a word to them until the next day in class when I told them the following…

"You know how much that car costs me right now?"

Silence...

"Nothing."

Tilting heads…

"See, that vehicle used to cost me $250 a month but now it is paid off. At first, I cared what people thought of me and that my vehicle defined me as a person, but I got smart and learned that $250 a month could become nearly $100,000 in 15 years."

"Whoa!"

"So guess what?

I'm going to drive that thing for 15 more years and then buy my next car in cash."

"That's really smart, Mr. Herod."

"Better yet, I do not have thousand-dollar repair payments like I did with my BMW, and the guys at the oil change no longer ask me about upgrades because they think I can't afford them!"

"I see you, Mr. Herod."

The mood was light and fun.

I told them: "Be careful about what people show on the outside. Cause their bank accounts might be hurting."

"But I thought teachers aren't rich," said one of the boys.

"Remember this," I said. "It's not how much money you make – it's how much money you keep."

I carried my head higher from that day onward and felt like I had potentially changed the lives of a few students.

Again, our brains are not wired to see long into the future. We do not like thinking about being old or imagining events that are not prescient.

It is necessary to see out into the future to better our own financial and general well-being.

Those lessons we learned when we were younger are still an integral part of how we need to behave today as adults.

Remember, only you can define your self-worth; not anything you possess.

Now that we're ahead of the pack, let's dial deeper into the investment industry and gain another leg up.

ADAM N. HEROD, M.ED.

UNIT 5
UNDERSTANDING
THE INDUSTRY

Advisors

Let's return to a burning question from earlier and ask:

How is it that the middle class can devote their lives for the greater good but receive such self-serving financial advice from salespeople hiding under the professional certification of financial advisor or financial planner?

Again, this is not to take away from those that are working tirelessly in the financial services industry to benefit their clients.

But what does it mean to benefit clients?

Like what we saw with Bogle, the advisors and firms are looking to create products that have a skew toward benefiting the client, while generating lower costs and maximizing benefits to their investors.

There are many different types of financial advisors, or salespeople, and there are always some that put their customers before themselves.

The problem lies with a segment of the industry and how it sets advisors up for bias – one that typically benefits Wall Street.

The term advisor sounds terribly official, but unfortunately it is rife with cover-up names for what is truly sales.

I would know as nearly crossed the finish line to become one, myself.

I've seen under the hood of the car.

It's true that many brokers and advisors are interested in doing good for you but depending on how they've been trained and how they are paid they may not even know the type of damage of which they are integral players.

In *Money: Master the Game*, Tony Robbins references a 2009 study from Morningstar that reviewed 4,300 actively managed mutual funds and found that 49% of the managers owned zero shares in the funds they managed.

What does this mean?

Plainly spoken, the cooks weren't eating their own dishes.

Were they trying to avoid a conflict of interest?

Maybe.

Or maybe they knew they could perform better in other stocks or funds without such high fees.

Whatever the reason, we need to take this information for what it is and not think so highly of others that are in control of our money.

It has never led to anything good.

Remember, 403(b)s are not covered by the Employee Retirement Security Act of 1974.

401(k)s receive more protection, overall; however,

And advisors, by law, only have to show they are working in your best interests. As you can imagine, working in your best interests has a lot of gray in its interpretation.

Follow the money and you'll find corruption, almost everywhere.

Everything from diamonds to even chocolate and avocados see forms of monetary corruption, so don't think for a moment the finance industry is saved.

The problem is we seem to forget that when the industry has a kind face and a recommendation from a coworker or friend, we think we can drop our guard and not conduct due diligence.

These are our livelihoods, people.

They know we willingly put our guard down when we admit we know nothing about finances or how to invest.

It's like walking into a UFC fight and admitting you haven't trained in martial arts.

Your accounts are going to bleed.

Who can you trust, then?

Fee-only advisors have the ability to look into your accounts and figures to make recommendations.

They can also legally advise you on specific investment funds.

These advisors do not stand to make a penny off your investments, because you're paying them a flat fee, so we can better assume their advice does not stand to serve themselves.

Coaches cannot legally discuss specific investments, stocks, funds, et cetera; however, they can give you an idea of whether your percentages are hitting the mark as you work to create an emergency savings, kill off debt and work toward investing.

If you need to get up off the ground and in a good position prior to investing, seek a coach.

If you're ready to invest, then seek a fee-only advisor or talk with a customer-centric institution like Vanguard or Fidelity.

Investment Strategy

Have you ever wondered if it is better to invest $1,000 now or $1,000 in small increments over a certain period of time?

For longer term investments, such as those using a Roth IRA, 401(k) or 403(b), **dollar-cost-averaging** is a great way to tap into the averages of the market without locking you into a market high or a market low.

See, we learn to buy low and sell high; however, we don't normally learn that kind of advice is related to buying individual stocks with a short-term investment horizon, versus long-term investing.

When investing for retirement, it is often better to space investments out and chip into the market one bit at a time, whether bi-weekly or monthly.

Sometimes your investments will go in at the lows and sometimes your investments will go in at the highs.

That's **dollar-cost-averaging**.

In the end, you'll have the average entry point across your investment lifetime and remove the poor performance of trying to time the market to buy at the lows and sell at the highs.

Our psychology often runs us aground when trying to time the market, showing that we enter and exit at the markets at the wrong times - as evidenced in earlier chapters discussing the internet bubble.

When **dollar-cost-averaging**, the likelihood gets higher and higher that you'll win as you also increase two components in your plan:

(1) the **amount of money** you invest
(2) and the **amount of time** you invest

Notice **market returns** are not a part of the components listed.

Ask yourself, which of the noted variables is completely out of your control?

If you said **market returns**, then you are getting the hang of this.

It stands to note, once more, that when investing in the market nobody knows the true outcome of any scenario, even though many have made money - often hand over first - overpromising on that very notion.

The truth is, the likelihood of winning increases with investing discipline and **dollar-cost-averaging** over a length of time - not chasing returns, as we've seen.

With the help of **dollar cost averaging**, an investor can:

a. Determine his or her goal income at retirement.
b. Project portfolio returns at 5%, 7%, 10% and 12% average market returns.
c. And plan for both worst and best-case scenarios

Wondering where to go for a. and b. above? Nerdwallet.com's calculators for target retirement income and 401(k) or 403(b) is a great place to start.

Input your current factors and see where you land, and then engage a professional to have all potential factors included in your plan.

For c., a **Monte Carlo Analysis** is one of the best tools out there to determine the likely outcomes for your portfolio, while including the above variables.

The simulation runs 10,000 portfolio scenarios and most importantly includes uncertainties within the simulation.

In the end, it will create averages across the 10,000 portfolios and determine results across different percentiles.

Remember when you aimed to be in the 90th percentile of your class - a top-performer?

Not all portfolios will end up at the top of their class, especially if fees are high and money is moved around often; however, with the comprehensive analysis done by a Monte Carlo, an investor can draw a detailed plan and determine if his or her portfolio is expected to meet their needs at or above the 25th percentile.

Vanguard, Fidelity and others can run these scenarios for you – often for a small fee - to determine the most likely outcome at your current investment amount.

You can also run your own on PortfolioVisualizer.com.

Just make sure you know which funds you're currently investing in or wishing to invest in before visiting the site.

The program will allow you to search up your specific fund, back test how the portfolio would have done across the history of the market, and even test potential outcomes if the market earns a specific percentage across your investment lifetime.

Pro tip: Always use percentages that are below average, such as 5%. This way, if the market averages a higher return over your investment timeframe, you'll have overshot your landing field.

"To the moon!" – Elon Musk

Using information from this analysis, you can better determine if what you're investing each month will stack up to your needs at retirement.

Then, you'll be better armed to determine if it is necessary to make any adjustments.

Monte Carlo Analysis | Example
80% U.S. Stocks & 20% U.S. Bonds

30 Year Investment	25th Percentile	50th Percentile	75th Percentile	90th Percentile
$200/mo.	$380,311	$544,283	$764,589	$1,033,751
$300/mo.	$576,484	$820,344	$1,149,560	$1,559,259
$400/mo.	$768,911	$1,093,820	$1,545,620	$2,076,872

*Gray denotes at which monthly contribution and at what percentile $1,000,000 is achieved.

Understanding Risk

When I began studying for a career as a financial advisor, one of the first things I had to understand was financial risk and where it would come from in the markets.

The skilled investor knows and manages more for risk, because he or she is more interested in retaining and growing capital, as opposed to losing capital to unforeseen factors.

In the lay-persons world, we hear the oft-mentioned, "Investing is risky."

When we hear this, we'll stay away from investing and growing our money because we set limits on ourselves that become unconquerable.

Don't fall into this trap!

"I'll never have a million dollars," we tell ourselves.

But Buffett would tell you the more you learn the less risk there is in your investments; however, most of us choose not to know - or learn - because life is simply too much as it is.

This is often understandable, and it is why we hand the responsibility of investing off to others.

If the investments fail to produce, then it's on them.

Has your mind ever traced this path?

For the purposes of jumping over that hurdle, let me lay out the main risk factors when it comes to investments.

Any one of these can bring the markets tumbling down, but often several them will correlate and work in tandem.

This is the part of our adventure where we're overlearning, so if this section is too much that's understandable.

Just work to learn a few of these so you know where your blind spots are!

Sources of Market Risk

- **Interest Rate Risk** - as interest rates rise, prices of stocks, bonds and real estate can decline. This has been a major concern coming out of COVID.
- **Regulatory Risk** - Decisions made by politicians and regulators that affect companies (taxes, legality, etc.)
- **Equity Price Risk** - the risk associated with directly purchasing common stock in companies
- **Business Risk** - how the core activities of the business impact your investments
- **Foreign Exchange Risk** - the risk associated with the exchange of foreign currencies
- **Credit Risk** - the risk of defaulting on debt by a company
- **Liquidity Risk** - how easily something can be sold to produce money
- **Commodity Risk** - the uncertainty of future values regarding grains, metals, gas, electricity and more

Accounting for all the types of risk can be freeing, as opposed to causing someone to freeze in the face of turmoil.

All businesses at any given time face all these risks and more, but as we've seen throughout the most recent pandemic there are safety nets and opportunities abound.

Also, regardless of which party sits in the White House, great CEOs have the wherewithal to maneuver their businesses through the many headwinds that exist in the economy.

And as we saw, investors with diversified investments – despite all risks posed during the pandemic – made a great deal of money coming out of the lockdowns.

Again, glass half-full.

What about the risk of not investing?

If a family decided to store $200,000 in a savings account earning 0.5% interest, that family would only have about $230,000 overall after a period of time.

And don't forget that today's dollar is not as strong as tomorrows, so their $230,000 won't have as much power in the future.

But what if they gained slightly more at 5% for 15 years investing in a stable fund that protected against the many factors of risk?

Their $200,000 would more than double to over $415,000.

The risk of *not* investing often outweighs the risks of investing, so build up your emergency savings, and work to invest the rest.

Keep a pitcher full of 3-9 months for emergency savings in an FDIC insured savings account, and plow the rest into something that will grow!

We're getting closer and closer to the road for wealth!

Markets and Market Returns

The history of markets and their ability to return on an investment are well studied, with an overall average return of 11% in the United States.

Whether the market returns 11% over your investment lifetime depends on many, many factors, including: politics, world pandemics, conflict, currencies, and interest rates to name a few.

In a letter to investors, Warren Buffet once stated the following regarding U.S. markets:

"In its brief 232 years of existence... there has been no incubator for unleashing human potential like America. Despite some interruptions, our country's economic progress has been breathtaking. Our unwavering conclusion: Never bet against America."

The problem nowadays is our access to information and the rapidly evolving nature of investing.

The information overload makes us focus on the subtle, daily movements of the market instead of the overall outcome in the end.

A study by Paul Slovic of the University of Oregon, presented in *Money: Master the Game*, measured whether our predictions of outcomes became more accurate as information increased.

What he found was a negative correlation between the amount of information and our decision accuracy.

Basically, the more we had access to the less likely we were to make accurate predictions.

Besides information overload, another issue that plagues us everyday investors is the fact there are few who desire to become wealthy slowly and methodically - enter investment apps such as Robinhood where investing transactions are quick and seemingly fun.

Emojis and confetti abound truly separate the contrarian investors in Vanguard and Fidelity from the Gen-X and millennial populations hopping into HODL (hold on for dear life) and YOLO their investments.

In fact, when COVID-19 hit and the world shut their doors, the amount of retail investors - or the uninitiated buying and selling stocks - grew immensely.

Suddenly, news, social media and even memes began influencing investor behavior, including stocks such as GameStop and AMC, as well as cryptocurrencies.

Some people made money, while most lost their butts.

Once again, we must be reminded that retirement investing and trading individual stocks have completely different methods and approaches.

There is an inherent peace in the long game, as we remain steady and consistent with the majority of our portfolio.

We can admit there is a lot that to be learned with maybe 5% or less of our net worth, trading stocks in an app like Robinhood or jumping into cryptocurrencies.

But most don't recommend much more than that, especially since trading individual stocks requires a great deal of research and discipline.

Retirement Investing	Day Trading
• Aims to make money over the long term, such as 20-40 years.	• Aims to make money in short intervals within a day to three days.
• Focuses on long term capital growth and research on specific funds that can beat inflation of roughly 2%	• Focuses on near-term news or hype, and involves specific skills to take advantage of rapidly moving stock data
• Can have tax benefits, including decreasing overall tax requirements within an investing year.	• Comes with higher tax implications, including the personal and capital gains taxes, which are charged for holding stocks for less than a year.

Not to mention, the ability to hold on or make an appropriate exit when you do not quite see the returns you anticipated.

As we've learned, investing studies show that people often react and buy or sell at the wrong times, which makes it tricky for those that dip their feet into the investing world via apps.

Our tether to our phones makes them less of a tool against the unbridled weapons social media and trading apps present to our base psychology.

There is an abundance of news out there that confirms our bias or is meant to create a scare factor, and just like going to the ATM after midnight never helped anyone, trading based on a recent headline may not always lead to the greatest outcome.

Remember, nobody knows for certain what will happen with stocks.

Typically, though, when everything turns green and stocks move higher people want to jump in for FOMO (fear of missing out).

When stocks turn red and investors see their total balances decreasing, they get nervous and begin to sell their positions locking in losses.

"Plan your plan. And stick to your plan."

Remember, if we want 95% of our investment portfolio to be stable then we need to hit the minimum monthly investment targets to grow our accounts and maintain those investments over a long stretch of time.

Refer to the **Monte Carlo Analysis** to determine yours, and remember that an 80% stock, 20% bond split may not be for everyone, especially those in the latter years of their careers.

Analyzing Specific Market Downturns

When the market saw absolute turmoil in March of 2020 due to COVID-19, people all over began calling their advisors telling them to pull their money out of the market.

Unfortunately, and despite their financial professional advising against moving money out of stocks around the market bottom, individual investors locked in major losses.

Had they remained in stocks for only a year longer, they would have participated in one of the greatest 365-day stretches since World War II where the S&P 500 increased by 76%.

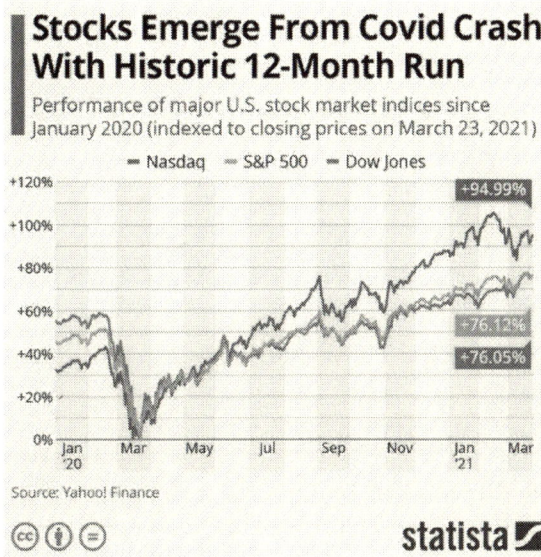

Stocks Emerge From Covid Crash With Historic 12-Month Run

Performance of major U.S. stock market indices since January 2020 (indexed to closing prices on March 23, 2021)

— Nasdaq — S&P 500 — Dow Jones

+94.99%
+76.12%
+76.05%

Source: Yahoo! Finance

statista

Figure 2 | Statista

The same thing happened in 2008, when in the third-quarter of the year massive amounts of money were moved *out* of markets – at the bottom.

In the end, it only took 1,107 days to recover from the 2008 crash.

Despite the inevitable recovery of the markets, time and time again, we find innumerable investors that cash out at the bottom when they've lost 20-40% or more.

Why does this happen?

We must recognize that we are not robots. We are an emotional being and that is why creating a plan around a low-cost fund, while **dollar-cost-averaging**, can be very helpful.

They tell us not to look at our retirement accounts when the markets dip, but it's terribly difficult not to do so.

You need a stomach of stone to ride the falls and come back up with the wave of recovery.

Investing for the long-term can help you remain true to your goals and keep you on the path – should you consider the temptation of deviating from the path along the way.

Plan your plan. Stick to your plan.

Bell-Curve Analysis for Funds

In his book, *The Simple Path to Wealth: Your Road Map to Financial Independence and a Rich, Free Life*, JL Collins offers up a great analysis for the VTSAX fund – and index funds in general.

He uses the Vanguard Total Stock Market fund (VTSAX), which was created by Vanguard in 1992 and holds over 3,700 U.S. stocks.

It exposes investors to the entire U.S. market, far beyond the top 500 companies.

Collins' analysis asks the reader to imagine all 3,700+ companies along a bell curve, being measured by their annual performance in the markets.

To the left of the curve are the lower performing stocks, and to the right of the curve are the higher performing stocks.

On one hand, a stock could lose up to 100% and experience a total wipeout on the levels of Enron, which defrauded regulators and conducted shady accounting practices to fall from a $90.75 stock valuation to 0.26 cents, when it declared bankruptcy in 2001.

This is a worst-case scenario that non-investors would point to and say, "See, that right there is why I don't invest. You never know when it could all go up in flames!"

Sadly, there were Enron employees that had 100% of their savings in the company's stock and nowhere else, and in one evening their money went up in flames.

Therefore we never put all of our eggs in one basket – aka buy one stock or cryptocurrency - or test the depth of the water with both feet, as Warren Buffet warns.

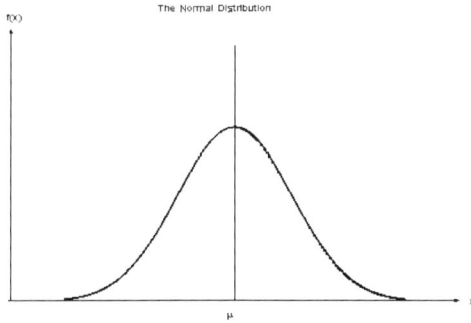

The Normal Distribution

On the other hand, what about the stocks at the right of the bell curve?

Can they counter a 100% loss by a company to the left of the curve?

The short answer Collins provides is: Yes, they can!

Collins offers up the possibility that a stock can grow by 200%, 300%, 400%, 1,000% or even more, generating an upward bias for the whole fund.

From what we learned before regarding relegation, the companies that experience the 100% loss will fall off the table, making room for new companies to join the VTSAX; however, the other successful companies to the right of the bell curve will progressively pull the fund further and further into the green.

As Collins reminds us, these conditions that inevitably benefit the investor disappear once active, "professional management" begins.

The natural, self-cleansing mode of index funds is gone.

All bets are off and, "They [investment managers] can, and most often do, make things much worse and they always charge more fees to do so," as Collins reminds us.

In an index fund, you effectively remove the emotions and the reputations that must be upheld when it comes to active managers.

No interruptions from the human psyche.

Just the market going to work.

In an index fund, you obtain diversification – investing in many different companies in many different industries.

If the financial sector sees risk from regulation, and stocks in that portion of your fund fall, the other 80% spread across other industries - such as energy and technology - might be fine and continue to grow.

Sector Makeup of the VTSAX	
*As of April 2022	
Technology	27.60%
Consumer Discretionary	15.30%
Health Care	12.90%
Industrials	12.60%
Financials	11.30%
Consumer Staples	5.00%
Energy	4.10%
Real Estate	3.60%
Utilities	3.00%
Telecommunications	2.50%
Basic Materials	2.10%

This keeps your investments safe, and costs remain low since the fund follows an index – something determined by a larger entity that requires strict regulation and success requirements.

This effectively removes all active management from the equation, something worth seeking for a long-term investor.

Now that we understand what to expect, let's get ready to **Make Your Move.**

UNIT 6
MAKING YOUR MOVE

Why We Invest

In **Laying the Foundation**, you identified your why for investing.

It was personal and it was motivating.

Always keep it at the front of your mind, and remember:

"Every dollar bill is a seed. Just as a tiny acorn contains the power to grow into a mighty oak tree, each dollar bill has the power to grow into a mighty money tree." – Robert G. Allen.

See, money doesn't grow in savings, and inflation acts as an undercurrent that continuously strips away the value of our money, year after year.

Like warm water under a glacier, if we put every dollar in a savings account, we will never see our money grow due to the erosion qualities of inflation.

And I don't need to teach those in 2022 about the impacts of inflation.

But remember how someone can turn $200,000 in investing into $1 million by investing little by little over time?

That does not happen in a savings account, even though that seems to be the safer option.

Once we realize the eroding power of inflation, we realize that a savings account is only good for emergency funds, and everything else should be in the market working its way toward growth.

This is where Warren Buffett reminds us, "If you don't find a way to make money while you sleep, you will work until you die."

Therefore, we invest.

How Much to Put Away?

One of the most important, yet unanswered, questions in most retirement plans is, "How much will I need?"

Most do not even get this far, which is a shame because we cannot hit a target we cannot see.

So we're not going to be most people.

We are going to get to the bottom of this.

In order to calculate how much we'll need for retirement, it's important to factor in everything from housing to food to healthcare.

Surprisingly enough, most do not factor in the ever-increasing costs of healthcare, including the need for more direct care, depending on one's overall health.

And it's important to recognize that it's rare for anyone to spend less in their retirement, even though most think they'll have fewer expenses.

Healthcare takes a huge bite out of your retirement egg.

Also, in any calculation, I prefer not to account for social security.

It's not because I don't think social security will be there, because if changes are made to social security along the way, it can remain solvent; however, I'm not confident social security will be enough to live on, especially since it is still taxed upon retirement.

This isn't a number we can pull out of thin air, so it's best to talk to a coach or fee-only financial advisor who won't try to push you on any products.

SmartAsset.com has a comprehensive retirement calculator that includes a lot of the main factors, including inflation, and allows you to know your monthly and yearly needs when it comes to retirement planning.

It'll spit out a ballpark figure of how much you'll need to meet your needs, and then you can compare that to your Monte Carlo likelihoods from before.

Amount for Retirement: _____

Or Monthly Income Needed: _____

Another general rule is to have about 80% of current income ready to go once you hit the retirement button.

Need an incentive to put away more?

A 2021 benefits study by Zenefits, a Human Resources software provider, found the United States to be the worst among developed countries when it comes to overall benefits.

Retirement and healthcare were two of the main variables in the study.

So if you don't look out for yourself, who will?

It Only Takes a Little

The biggest misconception we have regarding our path to $1 million has to do with the **Bucket-Spend Phenomenon**, where we fill up our bucket and that's all we see.

To become a millionaire, it's helpful to remember we do not have to save $1 million.

When we were younger and wanted to buy something that costs, say $20, then we were motivated to save $20. That sort of mentality sticks around with us into our adult years, as our goals change to televisions and Apple Watches.

However, with investing you might only need to allocate $200,000-$300,000 to reach $1 million, depending on returns.

Take the story of Ronald Read.

At 92, Read - a longtime janitor - died a multimillionaire and left millions to his local library and his hospital.

"If he made $50, he'd invest $40," said a longtime neighbor.

How did Read do it?

Upon evaluating his assets it was learned that he owned 95 different stocks and had held them for a long period of time.

He also drove a second-hand Toyota Yaris and lived frugally in other ways.

As we can see from Read's example, it does not take a six-figure salary to become a millionaire.

We just have to know where to place our money and stay diligent in our holdings.

Workplace Retirement Plans

We've established our disdain for high-cost annuity plans and actively traded funds sold by financial advisors.

Going back to our case study of teachers, school systems let these folks in with the idea of helping their employees, but most benefits departments don't realize how much this is costing our teachers, overall - a staggering $10 billion in unnecessary fees every year.

As we take the reins and eventually commandeer our own financial futures, one of the biggest mistakes we must avoid is failing to increase our contributions.

Especially as we receive pay increases.

Typically, those with 401(k) plans can automatically increase their percentages each year.

Whereas educators are often left to figure out our percentages on our own, if they calculate them at all.

Sometimes it just feels right to put in $50 a paycheck, but for someone making $60,000 a year in salary that only amounts to 2% in yearly retirement contributions.

Our goal is 10-15%, overall.

Calculating Your Retirement Contributions (%)

Yearly Contribution Total ÷ Total Salary = X

X × 100 = ____ %

ex.) $5,000 ÷ $60,000 = 0.08333

0.8333 × 100 = 8.3%

If your wage increases have been frozen, then you cannot be blamed for keeping your contributions at the same overall value.

You've been fighting off ever-increasing life costs and growing family needs, which is not easy.

However, if you have been receiving regular, repeated wage increases it should be in the forefront of your mind to keep your overall contribution amounts increasing in tandem with your wages.

Why?

Any good retirement calculator should consider wage increases, and those that do assume that your overall salary will increase at a rate that is at or better than inflation (~2%) throughout your career.

But let's say someone earning $59,000 a year is putting away 10% of their pre-tax income into a 403(b) account.

That's equivalent to $5,900 a year or $226 a paycheck.

If that same person receives a $4,000 raise to $63,000 and keeps the same $226 a paycheck, they will effectively decrease their contribution rate from 10% to 9.3%.

If that happens again and their salary goes up to $67,000, while their contributions stay at $226 a paycheck, they will take their rate of investment down to 8.8%.

Ideally, as the investor experiences wage increases, he or she can take a small amount off the top and move from $226 a paycheck to $242 and more with each successive raise.

This is the hard part about having to put the dollar amount by hand, instead of a percent.

It is a lot easier to set a percentage of 10% to 15% in the system than it is to type in $250.

Our minds see the $250 a paycheck and imagine what we could do with that money, instead of investing.

Once again, the deck is stacked against us and we have to overcome the psychological constraints set up by programs that do not entirely put the employee first.

Now that you have an idea of *how much* you want to contribute, it's time to determine *where* we should invest.

Most workplaces prioritize involvement in 401(k)s and 403(b) annuities, but most of these are the high-cost plans we discussed earlier.

Comb through the offerings to determine your options, but as we've discussed filtering out and selecting for customer-centric providers like Fidelity, Vanguard and Schwab are important factors in putting together your retirement plan.

401(k)

The 401(k), which is a workplace retirement investment program, takes a portion of your paycheck and adds it into an investment account in your name.

The advantage in the now has to do with its ability to decrease your overall tax requirement for that year. By putting money into your 401(k), you don't pay taxes on that money – since it's taken out of your paycheck pre-tax; however, you will pay taxes later when you begin deductions.

There are two types of plans to take advantage of: Traditional and Roth.

Most recently, pillars such as Suze Orman have advised employees to invest enough to meet their company match and then put as much as they can into their Roth 401(k).

What's the benefit? Upon retirement, all of the money that has grown in the Roth 401(k) will be tax-free upon withdrawal, as long as you don't take withdrawals prior to the allowable age without penalty.

No matter what, these plans were devised to encourage people to save for retirement.

Coming out of The Great Depression, not many people were putting money into the markets – understandably. Noticing a shortfall and a lack of sustainable inflows to the markets, people are increasingly becoming automatically enrolled by their companies.

As markets moved favorably through the entirety of the pandemic, Vanguard determined average 401(k) balances were up from $106,478 in 2019 to $129,157 in 2020.

It's important to know which plans you are involved in and determine your percentages. The 401(k) can be a great tool for future financial Security, but only if it is implemented appropriately.

Advisors are available to you within your workplace, a lot of times; however, they will often charge a hefty 1% or more to help you run your account.

Weigh your options and use appropriate guidance, preferably from someone who doesn't stand to make a dollar from *your* hard-earned income.

403(b)

The traditional 403(b) was designed for public service employees like teachers, but also includes other employees within the public service industry.

It behaves like a 401(k); however, we learned the 403(b) does not fall under the normal protections 401(k) investors receive, so we must be selective with whom we trust our funds.

The 403(b) can be a good investment tool if you are trying to decrease your current tax load, and as money is taken out of paycheck - pre-tax - you'll owe less in taxes that given year, just like the traditional 401(k) investor.

At the end of your investment horizon, and upon withdrawals, is when you will finally pay taxes. For some, this reality is not as acceptable if a pension and potential social security income will be taxed at retirement, as well.

This is where it's good to assess your overall needs to determine if it would be better to supplement your income with tax-free money, such as funds that can be withdrawn from a Roth IRA.

If you do choose to move forward with a 403(b), the automated deductions from your account become a forced savings that will keep you on target for your goal.

Within the funds provided by your institution, you'll mainly want to consider low-cost options that provide access to a wide range of equities and bonds.

You may also be able to select target-date funds, but look ahead to our discussion on target-date-funds funds and the overall equity-bond ratios we might need as we age.

Unfortunately, when Fidelity and others work with employers, the employer has the option on how many funds to provide to the client. Every workplace or corporation handles this discussion differently.

The institution might choose to provide a full book of offerings, which may include hundreds of investment options, or they might only be able to provide target-dates and some select funds that only give you a total of 10-20 select funds to choose from.

If you are overwhelmed by the options provided, customer representatives and advisors representing Fidelity and others are on standby and ready to help you choose funds to meet your goals.

Remember, customer-centric investment organizations do not pay advisors high commission rates and AUM percentages, so their fees are lower, and the customer representatives are not incentivized to push you into specific plans.

Naturally, target-date-funds will carry somewhat higher fees, and most people will settle for them because they require less work on their part, or incorrectly think they're better.

For example, the Fidelity 500 Index Fund has a 0.015% expense ratio, while the Fidelity Freedom 2065 Target Date Fund carries a 0.75% expense ratio.

Both are much less than the potential 5% in management fees the annuity providers can charge.

If you'd like to do a little more research on your own, you can see how your current or potential plan and the funds included stack up on www.403bcompare.com.

457(b)

The 457(b) is another pre-tax retirement option for public service employees. It is often referred to as deferred compensation.

Once again, money from your paycheck is moved prior to taxation and builds in an account that is taxable upon retirement.

Providers may offer fewer options, overall, but there are some unique differences that might be worth considering.

The most attractive benefit of the 457(b) happens to be its lack of 10% early withdrawal penalties, so for those planning to retire before 55 years of age they can withdraw their retirement funds without this knock to their bottom line.

Again, it is important to understand the relationship the institution has with your employer and the fees charged. Some will average 0.5% but be as high as 1-2%, overall.

There will also likely be a financial advisor that oversees the accounts provided. This person will stand to make a percentage of the money you devote to the account. So, as in any case, just make sure to do your homework.

Diversification | The Rule of 100

A snap-quick method of determining your allocations of stocks to bonds in your chosen in investment vehicle is to take your age and subtract it from 100.

Whatever your answer is equates to the total percentage of equities you should have in your portfolio.

The Rule of 100

100 - Your Current Age = _____ %

_____ % = Total Stock Exposure

ex.) 100 - 60 = 40

40% = Total Stock Exposure

Times are changing regarding this general rule, though.

Now into the 2020s, many financial advisors are recommending investors keep a higher proportion of stocks as they near retirement.

Why is the recipe changing?

Basically, because retirees will need the higher growth to compensate for living longer and the growing need - and costs - regarding healthcare.

Combining **The Rule of 100** with a brief assessment can shed further light on your stock-equity balance.

A free portfolio risk assessment can be found on Vanguard by going to **retirementplans.vanguard.org**.

They have several other calculators that are helpful, as well, but the point of the risk assessment is to personalize your overall preferences and punch out an ideal ratio that fits your risk/reward tendencies.

The Rule of 100		
Age	Stock %	Bond %
35	65	35
45	55	45
55	45	55
65	35	65
75	25	75

Determining your stock to bond ratio using the rule of 100 may be slightly outdated, but it's a good starting point to help you quickly determine if you have the right balance for your needs.

Diversification | The Buffett Estate Plan

Warren Buffett is famous for being a crusader against the active management model, as well.

In fact, in 2008 he was willing to stake $1 million on the fact that an actively managed portfolio couldn't beat out an S&P 500 index fund.

What were the results?

At the end of 2017, the hedge fund industry conceded defeat, when Buffett's plain old index fund had returned 7.7% versus their actively managed fund that earned 2.2%.

The reason the actively managed fund lost was mainly due to poor market timing on the part of the fund managers, such as buying at the highs and selling at the lows and the taxes and fees associated with all of the buying and selling within the fund.

Passively Managed Funds	Actively Managed Funds
• Track specific indices, such as the S&P 500 or NASDAQ • Requires less attention and less in overall fees • Seeks to match market returns, and often succeeds	• Create their own portfolio of stocks and/or bonds • Requires more attention and higher overall fees • Seeks to beat market returns, but often fails • Often requires the sale of products which involves brokers and advisors, further generating more fees

Effectively, the hedge fund moved too much money around too often, creating tax events and locking in lows while buying at stock or market peaks.

Buffett has made his billions by entrusting his money to true American growth, so it is no wonder he selected the top 500 companies in any given year to carry his money to the finish line, as he did with the S&P 500 index fund in this challenge.

If anything, we should look at this win by index investing as a phenomenal exhibition to which all of us regular investors were spectators.

Lesson learned.

When it comes to allocation, Buffett shared that he had advised his money managers to invest the money in his wife's estate plan at 90% equities and 10% bonds.

This is not the kind of advice you will often hear from financial advisors, because the ratio of stocks is so high.

Let's consider this one the extreme.

Using **The Rule of 100**, you would have to be ten years old to have a 90/10 split.

Silly, right?

We know most could not stomach the gut-wrenching and rapid changes that could come with a 90% stock portfolio and the onset of a market crash.

A dive of 30% on a $1,000,000 portfolio would cut nearly $300,000 off your top line in no time, and you would need the strength to look at that figure and not make any irrational decisions, knowing the market could rebound in due time.

Psychology says most of us would not manage this type of fund well, so it may be best to look for a better balance, overall.

It's simply not sustainable for most people.

But as we've learned, those types of drops don't last forever and the markets can, in fact, recover.

To verify the likelihood of success of Buffett's 90/10 portfolio, a Spanish professor by the name of Javier Estrada back tested this allocation over the past 115 years and found it had a real return of 6.5%.

In total, he analyzed 86 different 30-year windows and collected data on how likely the fund was to succeed and, specifically, how likely it would be to fail.

The **failure rate** identified a percentage for how often the fund ran out of money before a 30-year time window closed.

The rates are highlighted below for ease of review.

100% stock, 0% bond portfolio = 3.5% failure
90% stock, 10% bond portfolio = 2.3% failure
80% stock, 20% bond portfolio = 2.3% failure
70% stock, 30% bond portfolio = 1.2% failure
60% stock, 40% bond portfolio = 0% failure
50% stock, 50% bond portfolio = 1.2% failure
40% stock, 60% bond portfolio = 3.5% failure
30% stock, 70% bond portfolio = 12.8% failure

What did your stock to bond allocation come to using The Rule of 100 or Vanguard's questionnaire?

How does it do over these 86 different 30-year windows?

Estrada's data is only one set from which we can glean any insight from, but it is instructive to show that a balance of mainly bonds - or the 30/70 stock to bond ratio - does not necessarily lead to the greatest amount of security, since most of the fund's assets are tied up in the lower growth bond sector.

If our money isn't growing at a sound enough rate, as it often will with stocks, and we're consuming funds month after month in retirement, that's when the risk of exhausting all available funds becomes greatest.

If you're early in your investing years, a higher-than-normal stock ratio is worth considering in a supplemental account, but not likely in your core account.

Educators who might have a stable floor in a pension that is well-managed - to be determined by their state - and a significant other contributing to a 401(k) or similar account, might feel a little more comfortable taking a higher risk route with a 403(b), for example.

Especially if their investment horizon is long.

As we discussed earlier, the market will experience downturns, but those will occur over a short period of time.

Pullbacks are fast, while growth is long and steady.

The most recent COVID downturn took 126 days to recover and surpass its earlier highs.

Go back to 2008 and it took 1,107 days.

Further still and you'll find crashes in 1953, 1957, 1960, 1962 and 1966 all took about one year to fully recover.

If an investor has 30 to 40 years ahead of them, and there are four to six market corrections during that time, the corrections are likely to be short-lived and the account holder has a chance to recover prior to retirement.

But the key here is that one must be diversified across investment accounts.

Not all your accounts should have a higher-than-normal stock ratio, and not all accounts should be invested in the same types of funds with similar tax treatments.

It's about balance and diversity, while remaining comfortable in our exposure to stock and bond risk.

A Word on Target-Date Funds

We now know that our projections and theories on what will be needed regarding future income need to be fluid, especially as life expectancies increase.

To simplify the process, institutions created target-date funds.

These allow us to select the general year we plan to retire and then the fund handles the proportional changes of stocks to bonds as we age.

We can consider the subtle changes in the proportion of stocks to bonds as an auto-pilot feature that moves from stock heavy in the early years to a greater balance of stocks and bonds as we near retirement age.

The autopilot and stock to bond ratios will vary from firm to firm, but the overall goal is to generate as much capital while protecting from risk along the way.

And, fortunately or unfortunately, over 96% of large employers automatically default to target date funds for their employees, even though the funds might not meet the client's exact needs.

Many people see the target date fund as a set-it-and-forget-it type of fund, but this sort of mindset can lead to some surprises at the end of one's career.

What we have to understand is that target date funds only set the portfolio ratios.

They are in fact not set up to guarantee your retirement at the year you select, as some might think.

They can also still lose money, even though 57% of people in a study thought they couldn't lose money at all.

Key fact:
All investments have the potential to lose money.

Cutting Fees

We are taught that 1-2% of anything is not very much.

But let's play with some math for a minute.

To deliver on its product portfolio, Coca-Cola produces about 1 billion bottles in a typical year.

Hypothetically, let's say that in production they lost 1% of the bottles to unsatisfactory condition.

That means 10 million plastic bottles were wasted that year. Imagine 10 million plastic bottles stacked up, year after year.

If they were all 20-ounce bottles of coke at a rate of $1.99 per bottle, Coca-Cola would have lost $19,900,000.

1% doesn't sound like a lot, but can you imagine a CEO being willing to lose out on $19 million?

How about one more example.

What if you had 1% of the richest bank account in the world, which stands at over $273 billion for Tesla's Elon Musk.

You would now be the lucky owner of over $2.73 billion.

Any one of us would now probably take 1% of any billionaire's total funds.

Small percentages matter in the grand scheme of our investments, especially as compounding builds our accounts in our later years of employment.

In my personal story, I'll share the calculations for fees would have removed more than $300,000 from my 403(b)-retirement account over the course of my teaching career.

All for what would have likely been lackluster returns.

Losing that $300,000+ could have added up to 5 or more years of required work to my teaching career.

Getting it back through lower cost, customer-centric mutual funds could return years of repose for my target retirement date.

Focusing on fee reduction is an important task for anyone looking for a complete makeover on his or her retirement portfolio.

Fortunately, there continues to be a race to the bottom regarding fees, as institutions continue to find more and more ways to bring some of their investment options toward zero.

Depending on where you are in your investment journey, though, investigating your options in regard to fee reduction will be the biggest decision you make moving forward.

For some, it may be as simple as adjusting you're the funds *within* the financial institution you're already investing with.

Simply moving from a managed account to an index account could mean tens of thousands back in your pocket.

If you are already with Fidelity, Vanguard, or Schwab, you can do this yourself or call in to inquire about the process.

If you are with a payroll insurance company, as opposed to a customer-centric institution like Vanguard or Fidelity, then the process becomes more involved.

Key Point:

If you think it might be time to move on from your current provider, there are some serious considerations to make, as this will be the biggest decision regarding your personal retirement finances.

First, you want to see if your current provider already has lower-cost index funds, instead of a managed account.

Check in with your advisor and see what they say but remember to take everything with a grain of salt.

There is no real incentive to do what is best for you, even if they like you.

Compare lower cost index funds with the 403(b) providers at your school and see if there is a better landing spot for your funds.

Take some effort and do some careful calculations.

Moving money out of your current provider's funds is not always best for every scenario.

Always discuss your options with your current vendor, potential future vendor and a third-party fee-only advisor or coach.

Just remember a coach cannot advise you on specific funds, and if they do they are breaking laws with the SEC. Only a registered financial advisor can do that.

Remember, too, that each vendor has different stipulations around when you can move funds out and how much it will cost to roll those funds over to a new provider.

It's also important to know what may be required by the IRS, as well.

One cannot simply roll a pre-tax account like a 403(b) to a post-tax account like a Roth IRA without paying the man in the blue-starred hat.

403(b) to 403(b) rollovers are more common.

It's important to start by investigating your current vendor deeper and determining what avenues you have regarding who will take over your 403(b) after you move out.

Ask the following:

- **How much am I being charged in account fees, right now?**

    o Assume they are even higher than what you're being told – potentially up to 5%.

    o See if your provider has lower cost index-fund options, as opposed to active management

    o If you can't get fees below 0.5% for an index-based fund, something might be fishy

- **What is the surrender timeframe and what is the overall fee?**

- **Which vendors currently work with my employer? (For those in public service)**
  - o The money needs to come out pre-tax for a 403(b), so the vendor needs to be established with your district or state.
  - o If your district does not have a customer-centric vendor, such as Fidelity, Vanguard or Schwab, maybe you can encourage an introduction or get the ball rolling.
  - o Talk to a benefits representative or union representative and see if the institution can be added to the list of retirement providers at your school.

The biggest inhibitor to someone moving their money from one provider to another will be the surrender fee, which is what they will charge you if you want to move your money to a completely different provider.

It was a no-brainer for me, as I was early in my career and paid such a small amount.

I knew that money would come back to me in a short period of time, and the benefits of contributing $200+ per month into a low-cost fund for the next 25 years would far outweigh my surrender fee.

Someone who has been investing for 25 years and may only be five years from retiring has a greater weight on his or her shoulders.

Let's say you have an account with $400,000.

Then a surrender fee of 5% equates to $20,000.

Can you make up $20,000 in five years in fee reduction?

Let's take a look.

If your fund was charging you 4% in total fees, then for every $100,000 you have invested you are paying $4,000.

Moving to a fund with less than 0.5% in total fees saves you 3.5% or $3,500 for every $100,000 invested per year.

In this case, you'd recover $20,000 in total fees on a $400,000 account in a short period of time.

Every scenario is different, and the lesson here is that you still have options, even when you are in the waning years of your investment timeline.

Those fees won't just shut off when you retire, so this requires a scrutinizing look.

Key Point:
Make sure to ask for a rollover if you plan to change vendors, as you will not want to trigger a tax event.

Rebalancing

An often-overlooked tool in investment management is the portfolio rebalance.

When you rebalance, you go back to the original stock to bond allocation you most desire for your age.

Let's say you decide against a target date fund from one of the customer-centric institutions mentioned, and you would rather manage the investments yourself.

We need to remember that market conditions can skew us away from our desired risk proportions.

A 70% stock, 30% bond portfolio can become a 75% stock, 25% bond portfolio if stocks do well in a given year.

Now, that 75% stock number may be something you are not entirely comfortable with, since market dips would have a greater impact on your portfolio.

Fortunately, we can set up automatic yearly rebalances with providers, so our risk proportions do not get out of whack.

There is this notion of setting it and forgetting it, but letting your portfolio run unchecked and unabated could put you at risk when a downturn happens.

If we return to the failure rates noted by professor Estrada, our portfolios may enter entirely different failure rates, depending on how far away they get from our desired ratios.

Now that we know the intangibles to make our move, let's discover **The Ultimate Plan**.

ADAM N. HEROD, M.ED.

UNIT 7
THE ULTIMATE PLAN

Passive Investing

Earlier, we learned some differences between passive and active investing.

We discovered that passive investing often beats out active investment, especially regarding repeat performance.

It is unlikely an active investor will win in every market condition, whereas a passive investor will tap into the market's natural, long-term upward trend and refrain from the pitfalls of human error, emotion, and increased tax events that come from active trading.

But it still begs the question, "Is passive investing truly the best for me?"

If we are to truly stick to a plan and set our allocation of stocks to bonds, then passive investing may be more likely to bring our plan to fruition over the long run.

It keeps our hands off the trigger during major market events, and keeps our costs very, very low in comparison to active management.

Also, we must evaluate two specific things when making the determination of passive versus active:

1. Am I contributing a great deal of capital on a weekly/monthly/yearly basis?
2. Would hiring an advisor be overkill?

If you have a lower amount of capital to invest and you hire a financial advisor, the fees could eat into your principal more - keeping your account from growing much at all.

Hence, the focus on fees earlier.

Let's look at the outcomes graphically, using a $200 per month contribution rate.

The only variable we will change is the fees, keeping the investment rate, timeline of 30 years and returns of 8% the same.

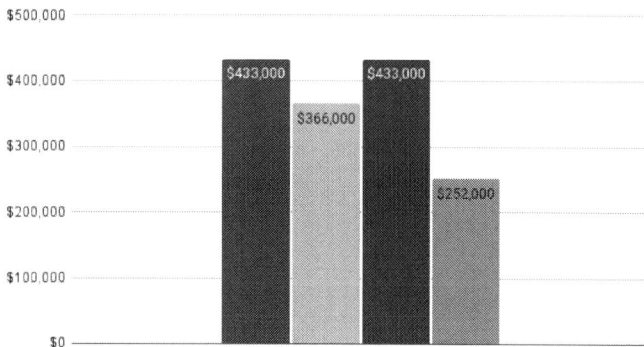

Fee Comparison | Active vs. Passive

After 30 years of investing $200 per month, you will see both accounts grew to $433,000; however, the "Total Balance After Fees" determined a uniquely different number for both accounts.

Remember, investment fees were the only variables that differed.

In the passive investment account in our example, an average of 0.0015% in overall fees was paid each year for an index fund that tracked the S&P 500, which took approximately $67,000 from our principal of $433,000.

Our final balance represented $366,000.

The active investment account hurt us quite a bit more, docking a total of $181,000 from our total principle.

This is nearly 3x the amount in fees paid to the vendor and brings us to $252,000 total in the account.

Can an active investor's fees be outweighed by higher-than-average results?

On a regular, repeating basis – not likely.

Jack Bogle | Financier for the People

Vanguard founder Jack Bogle was known as a financier for the people.

He was not out to take people's money, but instead vault them into returns and wealth attainment once thought to be so unattainable for Main Street America.

As the developer of low-cost index funds for Vanguard, he recognized everyday people needed to gain access to wealth building without having to pay someone else high fees for management.

In 1976, he introduced the index fund that tracked the S&P 500. This allowed investors to invest in those 500 companies all at once.

He advocated for people to realize they would receive the average returns of the market during their investing lifespan, and that the market average would truly be enough to become wealthy, given time and consistent capital investment.

One of the greatest pieces of advice he ever offered centered around the idea of returns, and he often spoke out against those trying to beat the market.

Unfortunately, the massive amount of attention the stock market has received – even today - has caused damaging results to people's financial goals.

He said broadcast television and radio shows were just there to entertain us, and - more often than not - caused us to overtrade and fail in the business of investing.

The business of investing being the disciplined, long-term approach required for wealth growth.

Overtrading, which became even more common during the pandemic, leads to locking in losses at market lows or buying at peaks when stocks are most expensive.

You recall this is how the active managers lost to Warren Buffet.

It doesn't sound exciting that most of us cannot beat the market; however, there is an abundance of peace in knowing that with the right, customer-centric and low-cost funds we have a very good shot at doing better than if we had just given our money to somebody else who would overtrade or try to beat the market and perform worse than a passive investment would.

Matching the market over the long haul could be the new "beating the market."

With the realization that we will earn the market average over our investing lifespan, the peace that is gained can free up our minds to focus on other things besides money.

This freedom of mind is the exact reason I was able to sit down and write this very book.

I did not have to check in on my accounts every week and worry about market movements, or feverishly listen to radio broadcasts and stock analysts to try and get a leg up.

The returns are going to be the returns for the period of time we invest, and if we choose to passively invest using an index fund, we are sliding our focus over to the two variables we have more control over:

- length of time investing
- and our contribution rate

The 2020 pandemic crash taught me everything I needed to know about my strategy and the acceptance of average market returns.

From February 2020 to March 2020 one of my accounts lost over 28% of its total balance.

Not once did I waver or put my hand on my account to pull funds.

By June of the next year, 2021, it had exceeded the prior year's balance by double digit numbers – all without touching a thing or changing my contributions.

Our plumber had visited at some point during the pandemic, when markets started to truly pick back up, and he had mentioned he had moved a lot of his money into a stable fund at the same time the markets dropped between February and March of 2020.

He was most frustrated with the fact that the markets had ballooned again so quickly, recovering from their hole in a matter of months.

His retirement fund had missed out on a great deal of growth, mainly because he had his hands on the wheel trying to outsmart the market.

The hands-off approach my account experienced turned out to be a 40% increase in one year, despite the ravages of the pandemic.

You see, the industry wants us to believe that we need them.

Industry jargon might tell you, "You'll lose money if you do it yourself."

Take it one step further and they'll have us believing we cannot feed ourselves a healthy diet, even though there is an abundance of science and research out there to help us - if only we care to take the time.

The investing world works in the same way.

With a little bit of research, we can take total control over our personal finances and even our retirement planning with viable financial institutions such as Fidelity or Vanguard as our guide.

The Handshake | I've Robbed You from Hello

Remember the question I asked a few chapters back: How did you stumble upon your financial advisor?

Most likely your search may have begun because you did not trust yourself or your significant other with your investments.

Then, you reached out to friends or coworkers so that you did not have to do any research; however, your trusted colleague likely did not perform any checks and balances either.

Pretty soon, an introduction was made and the rest is history.

This is called the handshake.

The advisor just has to gain your trust upon the first meeting, and they've got you hooked.

When you don't know all that much, who else can you really go to?

... so you think.

The trouble with us in public service and 401(k) investors in corporations is that we lack specific financial advice that is tailored to our unique financial circumstances.

For example, teachers chip into a pension but how much more will they need to have upon retirement?

Then, school systems permit financial advisors of all types into their buildings without much vetting - if at all - and we gladly hand over our hard-earned money each paycheck while they line their pockets.

401(k) employees have access to on-site advisors, but their role is to get you into more active management and charge a "small" 1-2% in fees.

And we have seen what even 1% can do to a retirement fund.

So if, for example, school systems aren't entirely checking in on the advisors, and you got a recommendation from your friend or coworker without much vetting, how many layers of thick cover must we move aside before we find out what's truly going on?

With the help of this book, the picture is likely becoming clearer and clearer.

A Note on Stock Picking

If you search well enough you will find examples of investors that beat the market by picking stocks, in an act of active management.

As mentioned before, it is rare that active managers will be able to repeat their performance.

That's why you've heard the very important claim, "Past performance does not guarantee future results."

In fact, if we track those with winning portfolios, over two-thirds of them are not likely to repeat their performance again.

Yet the business of investing booms when a fund manager does well.

For example, take Cathie Wood, CEO and Chief Investment Officer of ARK Invest.

Her ARK Innovation fund, a fund that tracked companies disrupting traditional markets, outperformed all other actively managed funds in 2020.

This performance garnered a lot attention for ARK.

In 2019, they oversaw over $1 billion in assets, but after their 2020 performance they boomed to $22 billion in assets under management across their actively managed funds.

Her business grew 22x in one year, because people were chasing performance.

In 2021, the fund failed to repeat their record-setting year as it was in the worst one percentile of all actively managed stocks by March 2021.

Who knows where they'll end up in the long run?

But we see once again the concerns about repeat performance for active management.

When the COVID-19 pandemic sent most employees home, we saw a cataclysmic shift in how businesses operated and consumers behaved.

Mad Money's Jim Cramer devised a COVID shutdown index, dubbed the "Mad COVID-19 Index."

In this fund, he included 100 companies he thought would benefit from the shutdown.

These included: Peloton, Zoom Video, Twilio, Boston Beer Company, Datadog and Cloudflare to name a few.

His "index" outperformed at a rate of 45% in comparison to the NASDAQ at 33% and the S&P 500 at 22%.

Again, it is to be seen how the stocks will perform over the long haul, as they were selected to perform under very specific market conditions during a very specific timeframe.

In the short term, it's hard to deny that Cramer wasn't spot on with his picks.

In reality, stock selection may be best left for a small percentage of our investable assets and solely with money we understand we may lose.

As we learn more about our personal finances, it isn't entirely inadvisable to place a small amount in what might be considered non-contrarian investments.

But, we should never use money that would take away from our regular, repeating investments into our retirement plan(s), nor dip into those funds to make up for any losses.

The Ultimate Plan | A Tax Diversification Model for Layers of Security

Below, I will outline specific ingredients for the Ultimate Plan.

These ingredients could lay the groundwork for the retirement of your dreams, but each plan can be built differently and percentages and investment choices will vary depending upon your tolerance for risk.

It could include a 401(k) or pension as its core account, but can also include the following: Roth 401(k) or IRA, 403(b) and/or 457(b).

Just remember, the 403(b) and/or 457(b) are only available to those who are in public service.

The goal of the **Ultimate Plan** is to diversify across sectors and nations, while diversifying the tax treatment of the accounts – whether taxed up front for tax-free withdrawals or taxed at the back end.

Of course, our goal will be to focus on passive investing.

The Ultimate Plan A Tax Diversification Model for Layers of Security			
Investment Vehicle	15% Total Investment	20% Total Investment	Details
The Essential - 401(k) or State Pension (if applicable)	8%	12%	**Pre-tax**; provides solid base for retirement; income taxes paid upon withdrawal No pension? Add this to your workplace plan!
The Tax-Free Add-On - Roth 401(k) or Roth IRA	7%	8%	**After-tax**; optional; acts as retirement account, emergency fund and college savings plan; **no income tax at retirement** **Note:** Roth IRA has limits for total yearly contributions.

Some investors might be nervous about investing 85% of their money in stocks and 15% in bonds, while another might wonder if they'll get enough growth out of a portfolio with a 60/40 split.

You can tailor your percentages any way you wish, using your prior experiences in early chapters as your guide or the advice from your fee-only advisor.

The key to remember here is that **time, capital** and **consistency** are your three best assets.

Compound interest can take care of itself and soon your initial $1,000 can become $40,000 and so on until you reach your goal.

With a six to nine-month emergency savings off to the side and all your debt requirements met, the path to a workplace retirement plan investing 10-15% and more can be laid out.

The Essential | State Pension or 401(k)

The essential state pension or 401(k) is the core of our **Ultimate Plan** if you are a state employee.

We remember it is not the whole part of our plan, because in the quest to become a millionaire, we now know the pension or 401(k) will only partially provide for what we want to accomplish.

The 401(k) was not meant to be the silver bullet to a healthy retirement, either. But talk to someone with a 401(k) and it might be their only plan.

Talk to your state or corporate retirement counselors and to gauge what marks you're currently set to hit.

This will be your foundation.

Many do not even check in on these accounts until a few years prior to retiring, but you can start almost as soon as your first contributions are made.

Determining how much you will receive from month to month will be an integral factor in determining just how much more you wish to put away in your supplemental investments.

The Tax-Free Add-On | Adding a Roth 401(k) or Roth IRA

Imagine you were a farmer, and you had the option to pay taxes upon your order of seed - prior to planting - or upon your harvest.

When farming, the overall objective is to take what would be a typical seed amount and achieve maximum yield – or amount.

Rainfall, soil content and nitrogen load can all increase or decrease your yield, and a farmer will inevitably spend more time tending to his or her crop than when planting it.

Knowing what you now know about investing, which would you choose to do - pay tax upon the seed or the harvest?

As you're likely discussing with yourself, it all comes down to the yield.

If the tax on the seed is going to be less than the harvest, then you clearly want to pay a tax on the seed up front, so you may reap what you sowed later.

This is the exact calculus of the Roth IRA.

Tony Robbins posed this very question to his readers in *Money: Master the Game* – should you pay tax on the seed or the harvest?

Scores of financial professionals have touted the benefits of the Roth, not only for its tax advantages but its utility in passing along generational wealth to heirs.

In fact, the Roth IRA - besides offering tax-free money upon retirement, since you're paying the taxes up front - can act as the following all wrapped into one:

- Retirement savings
- Emergency savings
- College savings
- Home (down payment) savings*

Those that expect to be in a higher tax bracket upon retirement love the Roth IRA.

How can you tell if you'll be in a higher tax bracket?

It all comes down to how much you're contributing to your investments now, or if you expect to inherit a massive windfall or annuity.

You will notice that any projections made throughout this book do not include social security, which can throw in another tax curveball - as it could vault you into a whole new tax bracket depending on your benefit amount.

With the general notion that the government will increase taxes later on as they cover expenses such as stimulus, infrastructure and debt, it is healthy to assume that even if you do not land in a higher tax bracket upon retirement that your general tax rate could be higher, no matter what.

Suze Orman loves the Roth so much she encourages 401(k) investors to put as much as possible into their workplace Roth 401(k).

She says not to go for the tax write-off today, as you're only putting more stress upon your retirement nest egg later on when you need it most – upon retirement.

Remember that your pension, 401(k), and 403(b) investments will be taxed, so if you think you will be in a higher tax bracket upon retirement then many advisors will suggest putting an emphasis on fully funding the Roth IRA, prior to investing in any supplementary programs.

The final reason advisors and investors love the Roth IRA centers around its lack of RMDs, or Required Minimum Distributions.

Let's say your retirement funds - even after taxes - meet your retirement needs and you are fortunate enough to have social security come in as well. If the Roth is not needed to supplement your income you will not *have* to take funds from your Roth.

Maybe you want to take $1,000 out during the first month but $0 the next.

The flexibility is within the framework of the Roth to allow you to do what you want with your money.

It can also be used to help with a down payment on your first home. So let's say you started investing in a Roth IRA early and need an extra $15,000 for the down payment on your first home, the Roth IRA can help you out.

The only limitations investors will face regarding the Roth IRA is its contribution amount.

For example, in 2021 you can contribute up to $19,500 to a 403(b) but only $6,000 to a Roth IRA.

The math around contributing nearly $20,000 per year to a 403(b) as compared to $6,000 to a Roth is quite a difference, especially when accounting for compounding.

There are also penalties if you deduct your earnings prior to age 59 ½ and your account is less than five years old; however, you can deduct your contributions at any time tax and penalty free.

So let's say you contribute $50,000 and your account has grown to $120,000, then you would only be able to deduct from the $50,000 in contributions or you would trigger a tax event.

But the notion you can deduct from your contributions is like packing a parachute.

It's there if you need it.

Therefore the Roth IRA can act as an emergency fund **and** a retirement fund at the same time.

The benefits are greater overall if you leave the money untouched.

But in the case of an emergency, you'll have a parachute.

Roth IRA on Overdrive

The potato chip, the ice cream cone and even beer and champagne are delights that were created nearly by accident.

And the rewards are oh, so good.

What does this book have to do with happy accidents?

As we now know, some of the greatest discoveries can sometimes come from accidental discoveries.

Mine started with a question.

One day, I asked myself, "How can I have my golf paid for every month?"

Then it snowballed into, "Well, how can I also have my car paid for so I can drive whatever I want?"

Mind you, these questions were not for the now but for the future.

They then got me thinking about Warren Buffett and his ever-snowballing wealth, specifically the portion that grows without him having to apply much effort.

I decided to research his dividend stocks having recently found Andrei Jikh and his debt snowball success.

If you are not familiar with **dividends**, they are a special order of companies that reward its investors with money periodically.

As long as you own shares, you will be paid dividends along the way.

But only certain stocks or funds offer them, so you need to do your homework.

You might be thinking; do they offer dividend-paying *index* funds with low management fees?

Oh, you're getting good!

Yes.

Yes, they do, young grasshopper!

Let's run some quick math. Let's say you have $200,000 in a dividend fund that yields 4%, you'd earn an extra $8,000 a year.

Some funds and stocks have different yields ranging from 1-14%, which is a percentage of how much they will offer against the premium or the number of shares you own.

Note:
Be careful with higher yields,
because they are often unsustainable.

So, get this: in 2020 Warren Buffett was slated to earn over $3.8 billion in dividend income.

Guess what he did to earn that money?

Absolutely nothing besides owning the right stocks.

That's right, he did not have to lift a finger.

Meanwhile, the CEOs scramble and work tirelessly to earn tens of millions.

Buffett is over there reading, investing, drinking Coca-Cola and earning billions.

Now, you are probably asking yourself, "What's the catch?"

If you invest in dividend stocks in a traditional brokerage account, you are taxed at a 15% rate and you will owe those taxes in mid-April of each year.

And you will be taxed even if you did not withdraw or use the money from the account.

What happens with the other $8,500, you ask?

Well, if you choose to reinvest your dividend income it snowballs and grows in the account on top of any contributions you made that year.

You remember the debt snowball to decrease debts?

The dividend snowball acts to increase your overall investment funds.

It only works with dividend reinvestment, which is a re-upping of money into your accounts as it is earned.

They pay out the dividends, but you leave them untouched – reinvesting them into your accounts to quicken growth.

Consider this option within your accounts or ask a representative to confirm you have dividend reinvestment turned on. It's a great way to create the passive income everyone talks about, which requires little work on your part, overall.

Passive Income: The money that's earned while you're sleeping, so you don't have to work till you die.

Just remember that even though you didn't use the money or pull it from your accounts, you will still owe taxes on those dividends since they're considered earned income.

So where am I going with this regarding Roth IRAs?

Here comes the good part: The whole premise of this book is to put people on a path to attain wealth and retire free of worry, and this nugget could be a game changer - especially when we consider that most pensions did not crack $50,000 in overall income for its newest retirees.

Then, that money is taxed, which means we get even less than the sticker price.

Let's say you start a Roth IRA account at age 25 and invest in the account until age 60. You are fortunate that the account returns 10% and you have now built an overall principal of $1 million.

Remember that this money is tax-free upon retirement, because in a Roth IRA that money becomes a 1:1 benefit as long as you meet the rules of 59 ½.

One dollar is one dollar, without the government sticking its hand out.

The Roth IRA is our tax diversification tool to help us supplement any taxes taken out of our 401(k), pensions and/or 403(b) withdrawals.

But get this: if you invest or rollover the $1 million into a qualified dividend-paying fund within your Roth IRA that pays out a 3% yield, then your account is now earning you $30,000 more per year.

What are you doing to earn this money?

Nothing, except investing in the right dividend fund!

Hello, Warren Buffett Jr.

The best part about this whole plan is that the $30,000 per year is without tax, as long as tax laws do not change from the time of publishing this book in 2022.

In the current tax environment, the dividends grow within the Roth IRA tax free throughout the lifetime of your investment and do not require the 15% tax payment.

Upon retirement age, you then take those dividends *plus* your overall contributions *and* earnings tax free.

Hopefully tax laws surrounding this move don't change after publication of this text, but do go ahead and double check as I am not a tax professional.

	Amount of Money Earned Per Year		
Principal in Retirement Fund	4% Yielding Dividend Account	3% Yielding Dividend Account	2% Yielding Dividend Account
$1,000,000	$40,000	$30,000	$20,000
$800,000	$32,000	$24,000	$16,000
$600,000	$24,000	$18,000	$12,000
$400,000	$16,000	$12,000	$8,000

Curious about putting your Roth IRA on overdrive? Look for low-cost dividend paying funds with Vanguard, Fidelity, Schwab and more.

This option is great for those that think it's unlikely they'll pick individual winning stocks like Mr. Buffett and others.

And – truthfully - the funds are a lot less work and the yields are the same or sometimes higher, depending on the fund options provided.

You can figure out how much you would make per year by locating the dividend yield in the fund and multiplying it by your expected account total or current principle.

Anticipated Account Total x Dividend Yield
= Dividend Income Per Year

$850,000   x   0.025 (2.5%)   = $21,250

Consider whether this extra income would push you into another tax bracket before you make any changes.

We want to do our lawful duty, but where we can it's important to save on taxes.

The rich pay oodles of money to lawyers and tax accountants to do this very thing, lawfully.

Now, if you are not terribly excited about the figure you have determined for your Roth IRA dividends, remember the amount of work required for you to earn that extra money.

Remember, if invested in a Roth IRA that dividend money is tax free.

Stay grounded in accounting for the amount of effort you would have needed to do in order to earn that money from a side hustle.

Remember, that this is money on top of your pension that can make up for any shortfalls or mismanagement by the state that oversees your pension.

This is a major layer of security that has now been added to your plan, and who doesn't like tax free!

Finally, you now know there are no required minimum distributions.

You may find out that you do not need all of the money in the Roth IRA to live well, and it can now act as a tool for generational wealth.

Worried you'll forget about this trick upon retirement?

Schedule send yourself a Google email for your likely year of retirement as a reminder, and title it, "Dividend Boss."

Remember that with dividend investing we're not as worried about share price appreciation.

For example, we know the goal with stock investing is to buy a stock at a deal and watch it grow to a much higher amount; however, with dividend investing the share price might not move all that much.

That isn't to say it's a bad stock or a bad fund, but we have to remember the money is being moved back through to the investors as opposed to upping the overall share price.

A Word on Matching

I've always been jealous of those that get a company match, such as corporate employees that participate in their company's 401(k).

This is something that is rarely offered to teachers.

When receiving a company match, as long as an employee meets the required minimum contribution, he or she will earn a dollar for dollar match up to a certain percent.

For example, let's say Rachael earns $75,000 and commits 10% of her salary to her 401(k). Her company has a 100% dollar-for-dollar match up to 4%, which means she will have $3,000 extra added to her 401(k) over the span of that investing year.

And every year after that as long as she contributes more than the minimum.

Most advisors call this free money.

I will always be jealous of that; however, with dividend those in public service have a way to win one back on those receiving the company match we might not.

Dividends are a way to be rewarded for investing, and if invested in a dividend-paying fund under your Roth IRA the extra money earned will remain tax-free upon retirement age.

The money you put forward in your investments is utilized and returned, so all you have to put on the line is the risk associated with investing.

The positive in your corner is that the companies in a dividend fund usually have long, well-published records of paying out dividends.

One can feel a sense of comfort if your retirement fund includes, for example, a Procter and Gamble.

They have paid dividends for over 130 years and have raised them for a consecutive run of 60-plus years.

Think of how many different leaders the company has had over 130 years, yet it still has the financial health to pay its investors back.

There are numerous other companies with the same storyline. Interestingly enough, our $8 million-dollar janitor from earlier invested in a lot of these stalwart companies.

Bundling them up together in a fund for your retirement, earning stock appreciation and a secondary, supplemental income through dividends seems to be a sound move - especially for early investors.

Adding Real Estate

Imagine not having to completely rely on the stock market for your investments.

If the market goes into a bit of a tailspin, you might be able to earn passive income from rental properties you own throughout your neighborhood.

And when you retire, your investment returns in your retirement funds may fluctuate, but your overall net worth is growing as real estate markets grow.

This time, it is not your investment funds that will determine your wealth but your properties, as well.

Time and time again, when evaluating some of the wealthiest Americans, they are either business owners with groundbreaking technologies or ideas, or they are involved in real estate in some fashion.

Simply put, there are tax advantages provided to landlords that are simply not available to someone running a business.

These tax codes act to enhance the wealth of those with real estate assets.

Basically, the IRS tends to treat landowners well because they are providing a necessity in the form of housing.

There are even examples of teachers and everyday entrepreneurs that have used real estate to break away from their jobs, as their income from renting property ends up exceeding their work as educators.

Find @lattes.and.leases or Grant Cardone on social media. @beardybrandon is another one that has done a phenomenal job at coaching others to master this sphere.

For example, in co-authors' Brandon Turner and Joshua Dorkin's *How to Invest in Real Estate: The Ultimate Beginner's Guide to Getting Started*, they tell the story of Michael Swann who found out his school district was going to potentially cut salaries by $12,000.

In a concerted effort for his family, he moved to quickly research how he could supplement his teaching income.

After talking with his brother-in-law, a mortgage lender, Swann moved into real estate with his first property that brought in $335 per month after expenses.

He continued to work as a teacher but started owning larger condos that brought in over $500 per month in revenue.

Soon, he started buying apartment complexes that garnered $20,000 plus per year, and eventually built a net worth of over $2.5 million at the time of publishing.

His income from rentals per year?

Try $160,000.

And he kept his teaching job.

In fact, teaching turned out to be more enjoyable because he didn't have to worry about potential salary cuts.

Reasons you might consider real estate:

- It costs nothing to make an offer on a house or a property, unless it is accepted

- You don't have to pay the full purchase price for a home – in comparison to an investment or franchise - and there are even options to put less than 10% down
- You can manage properties with a full-time job
  - o Worried about maintenance? You can hire property management for a percentage of the income you earn each month
- A property is an asset that builds passive income
  - o As tenants pay rent, they are paying down the loan for you and the property appreciates in value, which raises your overall net worth in two ways
- There are major tax benefits and write offs
  - o Due to tax treatment, $80,000 earned from a job will always be less than $80,000 earned from real-estate
- Built-in safety nets, including:
  - o Changing the rental fees to attract more buyers if you are worried about vacancy
  - o Selling the property if you need a complete out

Real estate is not for everyone, but those that generate a portfolio of properties and tenants tend to reap the rewards of their work.

Grant Cardone, author of *The 10x Rule* and *How to Create Wealth Investing in Real Estate*, admits he wants those phone calls about broken toilets in the middle of the night.

Why, you ask?

Because, in his words, that means he's the one receiving those checks every month - not somebody else.

And rent checks equate to income and growth in overall net worth.

A Note on Crypto

Bitcoin, Ethereum, Dogecoin, $#!& coins… 20 year old millionaires, Lamborghinis and mansions.

Where did I go wrong in life?

Along with the increase in retail traders moving stocks throughout the pandemic, we saw a parallel increase in cryptocurrency traders on platforms like Robinhood, Binance and Coinbase - to name a few.

Contrarian investors and baby boomers are abstaining, while younger generations have jumped in whole hog.

What should you do?

First, I think it's important to note where we stand with crypto at the very moment this book is being printed.

Earlier in 2022, President Joe Biden issued an executive order on crypto regulation.

This spurred a deep dive into regulating the crypto world.

Janet Yellen, Treasury Secretary, was quoted as saying, "There have been benefits from crypto, and we recognize that innovation in the payment system can be a healthy thing."

For you, the first rule in investing in anything, but especially crypto, is that we are not gambling.

As you gain knowledge you decrease risk, and we should never invest in something we do not understand.

Since most contrarian investors view cryptocurrencies with a dose of skepticism, it might behoove us to choose to do the same until proven otherwise.

Anything viewed without skepticism is unobjective.

As with anything, and especially when considering cryptocurrencies or stock picking, it will be smart to abide by some very important rules, such as:

> a. know your hypothesis and adjust accordingly
>
> b. only invest what you're willing to lose
>
> c. never invest more than 5% of your funds
>
> d. never tap into retirement accounts to fund crypto investments

A thesis or hypothesis is necessary in any trading scenario, and if you don't know yours you haven't done enough research.

Here are three initial questions we could ask ourselves in forming a hypothesis:

1. Are there any long-term applications to cryptocurrencies?
2. Which coin(s) will dominate?
3. Which financiers are getting in and why?

Connecting back to science - our stance on a subject must remain fluid as new evidence is presented.

For how long did humanity conclude that the Earth was the center of the solar system, only for that stance to be challenged by mounting evidence from astronomers in the Middle East and Europe?

After a 2,000 year fight, we now know - unequivocally - that the Sun is the center of our solar system.

If you're not a cryptocurrency expert in the slightest, but you want to enter the space, work to understand the landscape and determine answers to the above questions while remaining agile enough to alter your hypothesis as you go.

Relationships and families have been torn apart due to bad financial decision-making, and we haven't made it this far to throw it all away.

Mark Cuban, who we've referenced in previous chapters regarding debt, said the following about dogecoin, specifically:

"If I had to choose between buying a lottery ticket and #Dogecoin, I'd choose dogecoin. But please don't ask me to choose between it and anything else."

Should we apply this logic to *all* cryptocurrencies?

Should we apply this logic to *any* cryptocurrency?

According to a Quinnipiac University poll, 43% of Americans believe cryptocurrencies will be a major economic force in the future, but what is happening with institutions and adoption?

What about gold standard investors?

Visa Inc., Goldman Sachs, BlackRock and more are setting up systems and accounts for customers, and the move to adoption seems to be picking up steam as over 60% of investors plan to increase their cryptocurrency holdings, according to Goldman Sachs.

Second, we must remember that investing in cryptocurrencies is a lot like investing in a foreign currency or the U.S. dollar.

Have you invested in a currency before?

What makes you want to do it, now?

If you buy a crypto token at a certain value, will somebody else pay a higher value for it later?

Maybe you don't want to take the risk to buy cryptocurrency directly, but have interest in an ETF to spread out your risk?

The first Bitcoin ETF, BITO, opened its trading in October of 2021. It was one of the most actively traded ETFs in history, and it attracted over $1 billion in a matter of days.

Grayscale Investments, which is often featured on Bloomberg, has a number of ETFs available for those looking to spread their risk.

An ETF allows you to participate in cryptocurrency investing without having to worry about digital tokens and digital wallets, nor an exchange.

Lastly, a word on volatility is important here, as some of the greatest price drops (and increases) can be seen in cryptocurrency investing.

For example, in one trading day in 2021, Bitcoin dropped 30% to $30,000 and in the same day recovered losses to come back to $38,000.

How is its value determined, you might ask?

It is true that there is nothing financially backing the coin, but neither is gold backing the dollar to determine its value.

People value things for what seems like odd reasons, and if we go back to the core of value or what is termed "Value Theory," we simply have to determine why humans determine something to be good, approachable or desirable.

Nobody but you can determine how valuable cryptocurrency could be in your portfolio.

Could you achieve your goals without cryptocurrencies?

Of course!

I think we have more than answered that question in our previous chapters.

So whether it's Doge, Polkadot, Ethereum, Bitcoin or something even wilder, go into it with some good principles and a tilt towards stomaching volatility and an ever-changing landscape and you might even learn along the way!

Remember, there is no one-size-fits all plan for everyone when it comes to investing and retirement.

The Ultimate Plan can have portions taken from it and added to someone's overall plan, but it's always best to seek unbiased advice from a fee-only advisor – one who charges solely for their time and does not make money from the assets under management scheme, which pulls money from your accounts little by little.

ADAM N. HEROD, M.ED.

UNIT 8
PUTTING IT ALL TOGETHER

Depending on your view, wealth might be best measured in dollars.

For others, it will be measured in time, family or the loved ones we have in our lives.

Thanks to my father, I saw the writing on the wall when it came to my time here on Earth.

He taught me to seek a balance, because for years he could not.

And in devoting myself to teaching, I committed not to a get-rich-quick scheme or a 60+ hour per week career, but one that was paced and methodical with a healthy floor in regard to a state pension upon retirement.

I admit, at first, I detached myself from money.

Before I moved to my first real teaching gig, two high school teachers now friends said, "Welcome to teaching! You'll never have enough money again."

But as you can tell, I wasn't going to settle.

I was going to do what I love, and then work to benefit others outside of my role as a teacher, as well.

Maybe writing and real estate can help expand out from the solid core provided by my career in education.

Perspective is everything.

Imagine this…

If the average American lives for approximately 78 years, and the Earth is over 4.6 billion years old, then our time here against the Earth represents only 0.000001696%.

Our time represents only a fraction of the Earth's, and this big old rock will continue to be here long after we are.

If you need some motivation to get going, there it is.

Better yet, imagine each year of your expected 78-year life being put into boxes.

This is what it would look like.

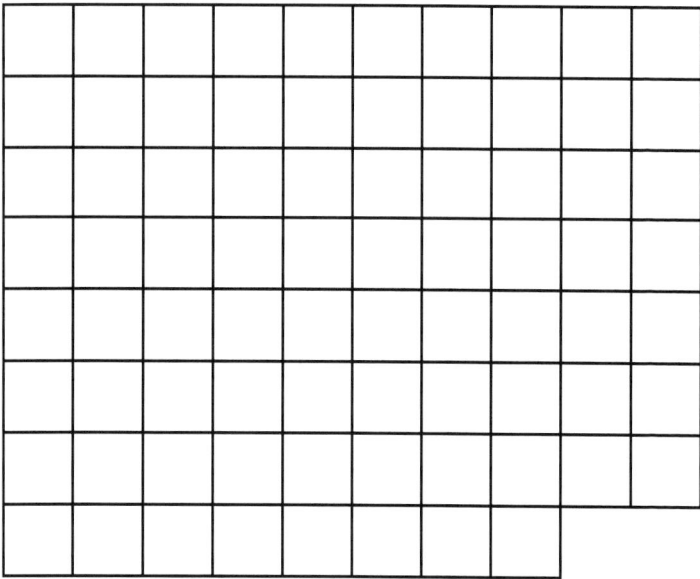

Go ahead and cross off the ones you've already lived.

It's a little humbling!

For some, these shifts in thought are saddening; however, if you have a growth mindset and one that can see the glass half-full, then a sense of purpose and motivation can overtake you in a hurry.

The question is whether that motivation will last.

With a sense of purpose and a determination to grow, we can awaken every morning with the goal of achieving our dreams of wealth and make them a reality.

I challenge you to comb back through this text from time to time or use it as a reference to start a conversation with your current advisor, or third-party fee-based advisor or coach.

You will even find a cheat sheet at the end of the book that can be quick guide to righting your course.

Thank you for taking this journey with me.

I sincerely hope your life and your wealth outlook benefit from even a few nuggets sprinkled throughout this very book.

Start now.

You'll never regret it.

And maybe you'll be one step closer to achieving the ultimate goal...

One Million Dollars.

ADAM N. HEROD, M.ED.

PERSONAL FINANCE & RETIREMENT CHEAT SHEET

o Start the conversation with your current advisor and determine you overall fees for investing.

o Explore options for lower-cost funds *with* your current provider, and then explore potential providers and funds with a customer-centric provider like Vanguard, Fidelity or Schwab.

o Use some of your extra time to hustle on the side and generate greater cash flow, or shop your resume.

o Speak to a state retirement counselor five (5) years prior to retirement

o Aim to save 10-15% of your total income into a 401(k), Roth IRA, 403(b), 457(b) or combination of these

o Prioritize your workplace 401(k) and company match, then blendin in some form of a Roth 401(k) or Roth IRA if you meet the income standards and believe you will be in a higher tax bracket upon retirement

o Look for dividend funds, which will help compound your account growth and provide passive income upon retirement

o Make sure your home/rent expenses represent 25% or less of our net income, or income after taxes

ADAM N. HEROD, M.ED.

REFERENCES

Picture: "Man Looking at a Rock Formation" by Tobias Bjorkli.

Introduction

Barone, Adam. "Teachers: Get Schooled on Your Retirement Strategies." *Investopedia*, Investopedia, 19 May 2021, www.investopedia.com/articles/personal-finance/112914/top-retirement-strategies-teachers.asp.

Kagan, Julia. "403(b) Plan Definition." *Investopedia*, Investopedia, 24 May 2021, www.investopedia.com/terms/1/403bplan.asp.

Bernard, Tara Siegel. "Think Your Retirement Plan Is Bad? Talk to a Teacher." *The New York Times*, The New York Times, 21 Oct. 2016, www.nytimes.com/2016/10/23/your-money/403-b-retirement-plans-fees-teachers.html.

Huffman, Eric. "Best Investment Firms." *Benzinga*, 21 Apr. 2021, www.benzinga.com/money/best-investment-firms/

"Employee Retirement Income Security Act (ERISA)." *U.S. Department of Labor Seal*, www.dol.gov/general/topic/retirement/erisa.

Frailich, Ryan. "How Not to Save for Retirement If You're a Teacher." *Teach For America*, 15 Oct. 2018, www.teachforamerica.org/stories/how-not-to-save-for-retirement-if-youre-a-teacher.

Norton, Leslie P. "The Annuity Trap That Teachers Need to Avoid." *The Annuity Trap Teachers Need to Avoid*, Barrons, 25 May 2019, www.barrons.com/articles/the-annuity-trap-teachers-need-to-avoid-51558743092.

O'Shea, Arielle. "Teachers: Here's How to Ace Retirement without Social Security." *USA Today*, Gannett Satellite Information Network, 29 July 2017, www.usatoday.com/story/money/personalfinance/retirement/2017/07/29/teachers-heres-how-ace-retirement-without-social-security/500979001/.

Aldeman, Chad. "Teacher Pension Plans Are Getting Riskier-and It Could Backfire on American Schools." *Brookings*, Brookings, 24 Feb. 2020, www.brookings.edu/blog/brown-center-chalkboard/2020/02/25/teacher-pension-plans-are-getting-riskier-and-it-could-backfire-on-american-schools/.

"Voya Corporate Leaders® 100 Fund." *Voya Investment Management*, individuals.voya.com/product/mutual-fund/profile/voya-corporate-leaders-r-100-fund.

Laying the Foundation

Loewus, Liana. "Why Teachers Leave-or Don't: A Look at the Numbers." *Education Week*, Education Week, 4 June 2021, www.edweek.org/teaching-learning/why-teachers-leave-or-dont-a-look-at-the-numbers/2021/05.

Kiyosaki, Robert T. *Rich Dad's Retire Young, Retire Rich: How to Get Rich and Stay Rich.* Plata Publishing, 2012.

Robbins, Tony. *Money: Master the Game: 7 Simple Steps to Financial Freedom.* Simon & Schuster Ltd, 2017.

Buettner, Dan, and Sam Skemp. "Blue Zones: Lessons From the World's Longest Lived." *American journal of lifestyle medicine* vol. 10,5 318-321. 7 Jul. 2016, doi:10.1177/1559827616637066

Pillars of Financial Knowledge

Kiyosaki, Robert T. *Rich Dad's Retire Young, Retire Rich: How to Get Rich and Stay Rich.* Plata Publishing, 2012.

Robin, Vicki, and Joseph R. Dominguez. *Your Money or Your Life: 9 Steps to Transforming Your Relationship with Money and Achieving Financial Independence.* Penguin Books, 2008.

Stanley, Thomas J., and William D. Danko. *The Millionaire Next Door: The Surprising Secrets of America's Wealthy.* Taylor Trade Publishing, 2010.

Robbins, Tony. *Money: Master the Game: 7 Simple Steps to Financial Freedom.* Simon & Schuster Ltd, 2017.

Figure 1 | Loesche, Dyfed, and Felix Richter. "Infographic: A Bigger Picture of the Stock Market." Statista Infographics, 7 Feb. 2018, https://www.statista.com/chart/12825/standard-poors-500-performance-since-its-launch-in-march-1957/.

Getting Ahead

Bach, David, and John David Mann. *The Latte Factor: Why You Don't Have to Be Rich to Live Rich.* Atria Books, an Imprint of Simon & Schuster, Inc., 2019.

Rossen, Jake. "How a 200-Year-Old Gift From Benjamin Franklin Made Boston and Philadelphia a Fortune." *Mental Floss*, 20 Aug. 2020, www.mentalfloss.com/article/627475/200-year-old-gift-from-benjamin-franklin-to-boston-and-philadelphia.

"Retirement Topics - Catch-Up Contributions." *Internal Revenue Service*, www.irs.gov/retirement-plans/plan-participant-employee/retirement-topics-catch-up-contributions.

Boesler, Matthew. "Almost 40% of Americans Would Struggle to Cover a $400 Emergency." Bloomberg, 23 May 2019, www.bloomberg.com/news/articles/2019-05-23/almost-40-of-americans-would-struggle-to-cover-a-400-emergency.

Understanding the Industry

Robbins, Tony. *Money: Master the Game: 7 Simple Steps to Financial Freedom*. Simon & Schuster Ltd, 2017.

Monte Carlo Simulation, www.portfoliovisualizer.com/monte-carlo-simulation.

Collins, J. *Simple Path to Wealth: Your Road Map to Financial Independence and a Rich, Free Life*. CreateSpace Independent Publishing Platform, 2016.

Figure 2 | Richter, Felix. "Infographic: Stocks Emerge from Covid Crash with Historic 12-Month Run." Statista Infographics, 23 Mar. 2021, https://www.statista.com/chart/20939/year-to-date-performance-of-major-us-stock-market-indices/.

Making Your Move

Elkins, Kathleen. "A Janitor Secretly Amassed an $8 Million Fortune and Left Most of It to His Library and Hospital." *CNBC*, CNBC, 29 Aug. 2016, www.cnbc.com/2016/08/29/janitor-secretly-amassed-an-8-million-fortune.html.

Estrada, Javier. "Buffett's Asset Allocation Advice: Take It ... with a Twist." *The Journal of Wealth Management* 18 (2016): 59-64.

Wasik, John F. "How Buffett Won His $1 Million Bet." *Forbes*, Forbes Magazine, 15 Dec. 2020, www.forbes.com/sites/johnwasik/2018/01/08/how-buffett-won-his-1-million-bet/?sh=2c14c5c22a6c.

Zach of Four Pillar Freedom. "Here's How Long the Stock Market Has Historically Taken to Recover from Drops." *Four Pillar Freedom*, 21 Oct. 2019, fourpillarfreedom.com/heres-how-long-the-stock-market-has-historically-taken-to-recover-from-drops/.

The Ultimate Plan

"401(k) Calculator: How Much Should I Be Saving?" *Nerdwallet*, www.nerdwallet.com/investing/401k-calculator.

Robbins, Tony. *Money: Master the Game: 7 Simple Steps to Financial Freedom*. Simon & Schuster Ltd, 2017.

Randall, David. "Analysis: Cathie Wood's ARK Funds Still in Favor despite Poor First-Quarter Performance." *Reuters*, Thomson Reuters, 31 Mar. 2021, www.reuters.com/article/us-usa-funds-ark-analysis/analysis-cathie-woods-ark-funds-still-in-favor-despite-poor-first-quarter-performance-idUSKBN2BN0HE.

Jarvis, Clayton. "Jim Cramer Said His 'Mad COVID-19 Index' Would Beat the Market - Did It?" *Yahoo!*, Yahoo!Life, 2 June 2021, www.yahoo.com/lifestyle/jim-cramer-said-mad-covid-132700662.html.

Leonhardt, Megan. "Here's Why Suze Orman Says It's Better to Invest Your Retirement Savings in a Roth 401K If You Can." *CNBC*, CNBC, 25 Mar. 2020, www.cnbc.com/2020/03/25/suze-orman-says-its-better-to-invest-in-a-roth-401k.html.

Burrows, Dan. "The 9 Highest-Yielding Warren Buffett Dividend Stocks." *Kiplinger.com*, Kiplinger, 27 Aug. 2019, www.kiplinger.com/slideshow/investing/t052-s001-9-highest-yielding-warren-buffett-dividend-stocks/index.html.

Dorkin, Joshua, and Brandon Turner. *How to Invest in Real Estate: The Ultimate Beginner's Guide to Getting Started.* BiggerPockets Publishing, 2018.

Launch of the first US bitcoin ETF: mechanics, impact, and risks. BIS Quarterly Review. Dec. 2021. https://www.bis.org/publ/qtrpdf/r_qt2112t.htm#:~:text=The%20first%20US%20bitcoin%20(BTC,in%20the%20first%20few%20days.

Books Cited Throughout Text

Bach, David, and John David Mann. *The Latte Factor: Why You Don't Have to Be Rich to Live Rich.* Atria Books, an Imprint of Simon & Schuster, Inc., 2019.

Collins, J. *Simple Path to Wealth: Your Road Map to Financial Independence and a Rich, Free Life.* CreateSpace Independent Publishing Platform, 2016.

Dorkin, Joshua, and Brandon Turner. *How to Invest in Real Estate: The Ultimate Beginner's Guide to Getting Started.* BiggerPockets Publishing, 2018.

Kiyosaki, Robert T. *Rich Dad Poor Dad: What the Rich Teach Their Kids About Money - That the Poor and Middle Class Do Not!* Bespoke Books, 2020.

Kiyosaki, Robert T. *Rich Dad's Retire Young, Retire Rich: How to Get Rich and Stay Rich.* Plata Publishing, 2012.

Robbins, Tony. *Money: Master the Game: 7 Simple Steps to Financial Freedom.* Simon & Schuster Ltd, 2017.

Robin, Vicki, and Joseph R. Dominguez. *Your Money or Your Life: 9 Steps to Transforming Your Relationship with Money and Achieving Financial Independence.* Penguin Books, 2008.

Disclaimer: At the time of publishing, the author is invested in and holds long positions in the following, which are also discussed in the text:

- Tesla
- Ethereum
- Dogecoin
- Bitcoin
- Coinbase
- Amazon
- Facebook
- Visa

Any discussion of the above is not a recommendation to invest or purchase.

ADAM N. HEROD, M.ED.

About the Author

Adam N. Herod is a personal finance author, educator and Maryland Realtor ®. After learning he would lose over $300,000 in fees to his 403(b) retirement custodian, he made it his mission to learn everything he could about personal finance and retirement – empowering himself and others to be in the know when it comes to money.

He coined The Million-Dollar Educator ® to be of service to others in their goals to build a $1 million portfolio.

Adam has a true heart of service and loves discussing real estate, personal finance and the road to retirement.

Find him @themilliondollareducator on Instagram

ADAM N. HEROD, M.ED.

Author Adam N. Herod, M.Ed.

Photo by Kristen Hudson-Nichols, The Artful Union
& Monument Sotheby's International Realty

ADAM N. HEROD, M.ED.

Made in the USA
Middletown, DE
09 May 2022